New Vintage

New Vintage

THE HOMEMADE HOME
BEAUTIFUL INTERIORS AND HOW-TO PROJECTS

Tahn Scoon

photographs by Anastasia Kariofyllidis

NH
NEW
HOLLAND

For Sassie

Contents

Introduction

Welcome to the second edition of *New Vintage*. Anastasia and I are so thrilled to have this opportunity to update the book with even more insider decorating and design tricks and tips, particularly on the subjects of colour and fabric—and we've been madly squeezing in photo shoots to bring you plenty of inspirational new images.

We really hope you enjoy this lighter, brighter and even more beautiful edition of *New Vintage*. A big thank you to all the clients and friends who opened their doors to us (and on one occasion even lent us their ducks!).

A BEAUTIFUL HOME
the bare bones

Sympathetic Renovating Tips

If you're thinking of renovating an older home, it's a good idea to research homes of that era so that you can form an understanding of which architectural features are original to the home—and should be preserved.

The workmanship and materials used in building many older homes are superb, and hard to replicate (some of those skills are almost gone), so it's important not to tear things out until you find out what they are—they may be of great historical and cultural relevance.

Certainly remove any poorly made subsequent additions to the original home, but honour and retain the architectural features that are precious—it's these details that give the home its soul.

Adding Soul to a New Home

Conversely, you may want to add more character and depth to a new home by installing traditional architectural features such as profiled cornices and skirtings, and tongue and groove panelling. Just keep in mind that most new builds are fairly clean in their design and any additions need to be too. Anything too ornate won't blend comfortably with the original design.

Another way to add soul to a new home is to use salvaged materials, such as recycled timber for flooring and cabinetry. It's especially lovely when it comes with its own history; for example, it may have been salvaged from a local wharf or town hall.

Life-sized statues, affectionately known as Isabella and Francine, recline around the 3.3 metre deep plunge pool, which sits within the original saw-tooth external factory walls of this contemporary home.

Materials and Finishes

Whether you're taking on a new build or a renovation, it's a great time to consider some greener, healthier options in terms of the materials and finishes you select. For example, most people automatically call a cabinetmaker to install new MDF cupboards if they want a new kitchen—but that 'new' smell you're left with is formaldehyde and other nasties off-gassing—so consider alternatives such as plantation pine plywood, recycled timber or EO (low emission) MDF.

For almost every product you'll need, there will be a greener choice, it's just a matter of doing the research (and avoiding the inevitable 'greenwashing')—and once you find the products you need, don't forget to stipulate no/low VOC (volatile organic compound) adhesives and finishes (or you may undo all your good work).

Walls

When renovating, walls are often the easiest component to deal with. More often than not they can be refreshed with a simple coat of paint and this is usually a job you can do yourself (the only exceptions may be if the walls are too high or the substrate too difficult).

Use low VOC paints to protect your health and the environment, and work with windows and doors open to ensure good ventilation. You may even want to go one step further and paint with a traditional paint, such as milk paint (see Milk Paint) which contains no VOCs (and smells nice).

If budget permits, wallpaper will make the biggest statement. If you're concerned about making eco-friendly choices, paper is greener than vinyl, which is covered in a film of plastic. You can even source papers manufactured from sustainable timbers and printed with water-based inks. Grass weaves are another good choice. Don't forget to ask your hanger to use low VOC paste.

Windows and Doors

The paint on timber doors and around window frames in older homes is usually oil-based enamel. Oil-based enamels are one of the most toxic paints on the market (which is why most companies are now producing water-based enamels instead) and they are a lot harder to sand back than wall paint. However, you don't have to get it all off; as long as you get the gloss off, it will be fine to re-paint. If you'd like to re-paint with a water-based enamel, use an all-purpose acrylic primer first.

Good painting is all in the preparation; so don't skimp on the sanding no matter how tedious. Also, keep in mind that most paints manufactured before 1970 contained lead—so before sanding anything in an older house, buy a lead-testing kit (very cheap and easy to use, and available at big hardware stores) and check for lead first.

Aluminium windows and doorframes can be a little trickier to beautify. If you have the money, add character to the home by replacing them with beautiful salvaged pieces. I've seen internal bedroom doors replaced with vintage 'Powder Room' doors salvaged from a ladies' restroom and aluminium sliding doors replaced with old red, timber shop doors—it looks fabulous.

However, if your budget doesn't allow for replacements, aluminium frames can be painted out in the same colour as the architraves so they become less obvious. White frames on white architraves and walls work particularly well. Aluminium needs to be prepared properly before painting. You'll need to rough the frames back with a scouring pad and then apply an adhesive primer.

Floors

When it comes to flooring, it's often most desirable to work with what you have. If you're lucky enough to rip up old carpet to reveal hardwood floorboards—simply have them sanded, re-stained (if needed) and sealed. Though you can save a little money by hiring a sander and sanding back the floors yourself, it's often not worth the risk of damaging the timber—hardwood is precious and can only be sanded so many times.

Freshly stained and raw floorboards need to be sealed for durability. Avoid solvent-based polyurethane coatings as most are extremely toxic (and banned in parts of Europe and the US) and opt for low VOC water-based polyurethane coatings instead. Water-based coatings also tend to look more natural and less shiny or 'plastic'. Seek out companies that specialise in healthier, eco-friendly finishes.

Alternatively, seal floors with an eco-friendly hard wax oil. Though this is a slightly more expensive option, the finish is absolutely divine as the hard wax oil penetrates and treats the timber, bringing out all of its natural beauty and patina. The finish is soft and tactile with a 'hand-done' quality to it. It's completely non-toxic, 100 per cent natural and sourced from renewable resources.

Other options are to apply tung oil or a beeswax polish. However, Tung Oil is petroleum-based and contains harmful chemicals (it can be particularly bothersome for those with asthma), and a beeswax polish won't permanently seal the floors, so they'll need to be re-done very regularly.

If you have softwood floors, such as pine, you may want to disguise the yellowness of the timber. You can do this by applying a deep, cool-brown timber stain to create darker floors—or you might like to try a white wood-wash for a fresh Scandinavian style. (Just keep in mind that wood-washes soak into the timber, so once they're on, they're quite hard to get off again.)

If you have dated ceramic tiles, consider ripping them up and diamond polishing the raw concrete slab for a more industrial look (see The Kitchen). Alternatively, if tiles are in good condition, you could save on the cost of having them ripped up by laying new tiles or floating a timber floor directly over the existing tiles.

If you are laying new floors, keep in mind your most eco-friendly options are bamboo, cork, recycled and forest-friendly timbers and natural fibres such as sisal and jute.

Hardwood floors sealed with a water-based polyurethane coating.

Affordable Updates for Kitchens and Bathrooms

When renovating, it's most often the bathroom and kitchen we want to rip out and replace. However, if your budget doesn't allow for a new bathroom and kitchen, try these simple, affordable updates instead.

- To affordably update a bathroom, paint, rather than tile, bathroom walls: it will save you a fortune. Use a satin finish acrylic as it will handle moisture and discourage mould growth (if mould is already a problem, clean first with a diluted clove oil solution—mix one teaspoon of clove oil with one litre of water into a spray bottle, spray on and leave for a few hours before washing off—then add a couple of drops of mould killer to your paint to prevent regrowth. If this natural remedy doesn't work, bleach will).

- Revamp old tiles by replacing damaged, discoloured grout. This is fairly easy—carefully remove the old grout with a toothed carbide grit-edge cutting blade, vacuum away the dust, then wash with warm water and vinegar. Apply the new grout, leave to set and then seal.

- Update an old toilet by simply replacing the toilet seat. In most cases the seat will be a standard size and it'll be an easy do-it-yourself project—however, some older toilets won't fit today's standard-sized seats, so check first by measuring the distance between the two back screws which attach the toilet seat to the toilet bowl and the width and length of the bowl.

- Convert an old single flush toilet into a dual flush toilet by buying a simple water-saving device, which you can install yourself in just a few minutes—miles cheaper than replacing the whole toilet.

- Instead of going to the expense of replacing or re-enamelling a chipped tub or vanity, apply a coat of epoxy enamel to achieve a smooth, fresh finish.

- If you can't afford top-end designer taps, buy the cheaper versions available at hardware stores. If you keep to the simpler styles, you won't even be able to tell the difference. However, not too cheap, they still need to work well—and keep in mind stainless steel is a more environmental choice than chrome.

- A new shower screen will instantly freshen a tired bathroom and will make it appear larger. Again, buy from one of the larger hardware stores to get a good price. If you have some do-it-yourself experience, you may even be able to save on the installation fee. Alternatively, the most affordable option of all is a fresh, white shower curtain.

- The best way of affordably updating a kitchen is to leave the internal cabinetry intact and just revamp or replace the doors, hardware and bench tops.

- Outdated laminate cupboard doors can be painted—the trick is to use a specialised primer and then apply the paint with small mohair rollers so as to not leave brush marks. However, the result isn't wonderful so a better option is to replace the doors. If you're lucky enough to have standard door sizes, simply unscrew the old doors and replace with the new, which can be bought from the likes of IKEA.

- Replace old, unattractive cupboard knobs and handles with new ones. Hardware stores sell handles quite cheaply. To save you from having to fill old holes and re-drill new ones, take one of your old handles with you when you go shopping so that you can match up the size.

- If you're lucky enough to have removable, laminate bench tops you may be able to update them very affordably. Check to see whether the bench tops are secured by screws running up through the cabinets. If they are, they should be easy to un-screw and replace.

- Consider using pressed tin metal panels or IKEA reversible laminated wall panels, rather than tiles—both are cheaper and easier to install. Salvaged tiles are another cost-saving option.

- Source a large second-hand butcher's block to use in lieu of an island bench. Revamp with a dark stain or a coat of paint, and add a linen skirt instead of cupboard doors.

- If the cabinetry is beyond repair and needs to be replaced consider a kit kitchen. This will usually be around half the price of a bespoke kitchen. However, they can be tricky to install. A good tip is to pay a professional to check floor and wall levels before installation.

- Alternatively, source a second-hand kitchen from your local dealer or online.

- Your cheapest bench top option is usually laminate but if you have your heart set on stone, order directly through a stone mason rather than through your kitchen supplier—you'll save a considerable amount of money.

Case Study

When Anastasia and her husband Jason moved into their 1950s brick cavity home the kitchen was an eyesore and the bathroom was covered in black mould. As they were working on a tight budget, they came up with some ingenious solutions.

The kitchen was striped back and all the old MDF cabinetry was ripped out. To avoid the cost of new cabinetry, a freestanding stainless steel bench and freestanding timber cupboards and island were sourced. The plumbing remained in the same location and pressed tin panels were spray painted by Jason and used in lieu of splashback tiles. The kitchen, excluding appliances, came in under US$5200/£3,392.

In the bathroom, the dated ceramic tiles were ripped up to reveal the original hardwood floors, which were sanded and sealed—the wall tiles removed and the walls painted (with the exception of the one concrete wall, they loved the colour and finish, so simply sealed rather than painted)—and a new bath and vanity installed. Painting rather than tiling, not moving the location of the plumbing and Jason undertaking some of the labour himself were the biggest cost savers. The entire bathroom came in at under US$2000/£1304.

Opposite: After—Anastasia and Jason's bathroom.

Cooling and Heating Your Home

The most effective way to keep your home cool is to insulate it adequately. You can save up to 45 per cent on energy used for cooling by adding roof and ceiling insulation, and a further 20 per cent by insulating the walls. The addition of a roof ventilation system, such as a whirly-bird, will expel any hot air that does accumulate.

Cross ventilation is also important. Track the movement of breezes through your home and determine if there are any obstructions. Enclosed verandas may be opened up, solid garden walls replaced with lattice, or windows added to allow the breeze through. In the absence of breezes, personal and ceiling fans can be used to create air movement and assist ventilation. Ceiling fans in particular are incredibly energy efficient and can cut the need for air-conditioning by more than half.

Air-conditioners are cost intensive, both financially and environmentally, and it is best to use them efficiently. Avoid installing air-conditioners in high indoor-outdoor traffic zones; instead place in the one or two rooms that will benefit the most and keep windows and doors closed while running.

Windows can be the greatest source of unwanted heat gain into a home. To prevent the penetration of this heat, glass must be protected. While heavy curtains and close-fitting blinds certainly offer good relief, the most effective means is by shading externally. Direct sun can radiate as much energy as a single-bar heater. Shading can block up to 90 per cent of this heat. External shading options include pergolas, shutters, eaves, verandas and planting. Clever planting is fabulous because it adds good looks to your home as well. Trees with high canopies will block the high summer sun on the northern aspect (in the southern hemisphere), but allow the lower winter sun through. Alternatively, deciduous trees could be used for the same purpose. On the east and west, lower, thicker trees and shrubs will stop the low angled sun from penetrating. Again, deciduous varieties could be used if winter sun was desired.

If external shading devices are not an option due to lack of access, or the unwillingness to block a view, treated glass (such as toned, or low-E) or the use of a reflective coating will help to keep radiant heat out.

The exterior colour of your home should be light to reflect the heat and keep the temperature down inside. Up to one-third of all unwanted heat comes in through the roof, so it is particularly important to avoid a dark coloured roof. Light colours make us feel cooler psychologically and are physically cooler to touch. Pavers, therefore, need to be a light colour. However, light-coloured pavers outside north-facing windows may reflect unwanted glare into the home, so try planting a good ground cover instead.

Insulation works both ways, so all the suggestions for cooling, also work for heating. In addition, use a feather to track down the source of any draughts and fill any cracks or gaps in skirting boards, walls and joins with filler. Place fabric snakes under doorways, lay thick rugs on bare floors and close up unused milk and mail chutes.

As with cooling, the right window treatments are very important. To keep heat in use thick, tight-fitting curtains and add pelmets—blinds and timber venetians won't keep the heat in very effectively. While in summer it's wise to keep the curtains closed during the day to keep the heat out, in winter it's more desirable to leave the curtains open to allow the heat in (but remember to close them once the sun goes down to retain the warmth). In very cold climes, you may need to consider double or even triple glazing.

Traditional fireplaces are romantic, but unfortunately not that great for the environment or our health (they can produce carbon monoxide, among other pollutants). They're also notoriously inefficient as around 85 per cent of the heat escapes up the chimney. However, there are now new contemporary slow-combustion fireplaces on the market, which heat more efficiently with less pollution.

If you have high ceilings, you may find a lot of your heat sits up near the ceiling; install a ceiling fan to help distribute it more evenly around the room.

The Importance of Good Air Quality

It's a little disarming to realise that sometimes the air inside your home can be more polluted than the air outside. However, by selecting the right materials and products to use in your home and by allowing plenty of fresh air and good ventilation (and a few high-performing plants)—you can have a home that is as healthy as it is beautiful.

Furniture

Reduce your family's exposure to formaldehyde by avoiding furniture made with pressed wood products such as fibreboard (MDF), particleboard and plywood—all of which use formaldehyde as a binding agent. Instead opt for eco-furniture constructed from plantation or recycled timbers, or timber alternatives, such as bamboo.

If you have existing MDF furniture, seal any exposed ends with a coat of milk paint or shellac. Alternatively, try EO particleboard, which has all the practicality of other particleboards but emits much lower levels of formaldehyde.

Another good option is vintage furniture: it's either finished with natural shellac and beeswax or it's already 'off-gassed' years ago.

Paint

Most commercial paints on the market contain all sorts of harmful chemicals know as VOCs (volatile organic compounds). The worst offenders are oil-based enamels, which should be avoided where possible (up to 60 per cent VOCs). Water-based paints have much lower levels of VOCs but care should still be taken when painting. Never let anyone, particularly a child, sleep in a freshly painted room—air it out thoroughly until all the 'new paint' smell has gone.

An even better option is to avoid the smell, and therefore the chemicals, by using natural paints containing no VOCs.

Fabrics

When buying bed linen, choose natural fibres as they work in harmony with the body; regulating temperature and allowing skin to breath. The best choices are linen, wool, hemp and organic cotton. (Conventional cotton growers use staggering amounts of pesticides.).

Similarly, select mattresses made with as many natural fibres as possible—and avoid synthetic foam mattresses as they emit formaldehyde and other chemicals. Also avoid permanent press and stain-protected fabrics for drapery and upholstery for similar reasons. Opt for natural linens and cottons instead: they will stain more easily but you can counteract that a little by choosing pre-shrunk washable fabrics, which are easy to clean. Protect upholstered furniture with washable slipcovers.

Floors

Carpet can be wonderfully comforting in the bedroom—however, synthetic carpets contain all sorts of chemical nasties, so choose pure wool with natural jute backing and have it tacked into place instead of glued.

For those with asthma or other allergies, it is best to avoid carpet all together as it harbours dust mites, which can trigger attacks. Timber, bamboo or linoleum (made from linseed) floors are the healthiest and most environmentally friendly—but be mindful of what glues and finishes are used.

If you choose timber floors, avoid harsh chemical sealers and stains; instead, seek out natural oils, waxes and plant-based floor vanishes.

Plants

It's well known that plants convert carbon dioxide to oxygen, but less well known that they also absorb and store pollutants—therefore adding plants to the bedroom is a simple, natural way to instantly improve air quality.

The best plants are those with broad leafs and strong root systems, as they are better able to absorb more pollutants. Studies carried out at NASA named the peace lily and tropical palms as being the most effective. The University of Technology in Sydney backed this up when they discovered that kentia palms, placed in an enclosed room, eliminated benzene, a known carcinogen, by 90 per cent after only 24 hours.

For Good Measure

Here are some standard measurements, which may come in handy.

Furniture and Cabinetry

- Dining Table—Average width, 35½ in (100 cm). You need about 24 in (60 cm) in length for each diner and at least 32 in (80 cm) of space between the table and wall to allow for chairs to be pulled out.
- Kitchen and Island Benches—Kitchen benches are generally 36 in (90 cm) high; however, you may want to go higher if you're taller. Island benches are usually the same height, but go lower if you bake/cook a lot, as 32 in (80 cm) is a better height for kneading, chopping and mixing. Barstools need to be 12 in (30 cm) lower than the counter.
- Sofas—The average three-seat sofa is 80–92 x 36 in (200–230 x 90 cm) deep; the average two-seat, 72–76 x 36 in (180–190 x 90 cm) deep; and a single seat, 36–40 x 36 in (90–100 x 90 cm) deep. The coffee table should be around the same height as the sofa and placed around 20 in (50 cm) away.
- Beds—A king size bed is 73 x 81 in (183 x 203 cm); queen 61 x 81 in (153 x 203 cm); double 55 x 75 in (137 x 187 cm); king single 42.5 x 81 in (106 x 203 cm) and a single 37 x 75 in (92 x 187 cm). Bedside tables should be the same height as the top of the mattress and lamps no higher than the top of the bedhead.

Distances and Heights

- The television should be at approximately three times the screen width away from viewers.
- A chandelier should be hung at least 30 in (75 cm) off the table.
- The average ceiling height is 7 ft 10.5 in (2.4 m), but 8 ft 10.3 in high (2.7 m) ceilings create a greater sense of opulence.
- The average door height is 6 ft 10.7 in (2.1 m), but in a new build, go higher to create an illusion of more space.
- When placing furniture, walkways need to be at least 3 ft 3.37 in (1 m) wide.
- A bedroom needs to be at least 16 ft 4.85 in (5 x 5 m) to accommodate a king size bed.
- A kitchen needs to be at least 7 ft 10.5 in x 11 ft 5.8 in (2.4 x 3.5 m) to comfortably accommodate an island bench.

Good Lighting

During the day a home needs plenty of good natural light. If your home doesn't have enough, consider installing a skylight, replacing solid internal doors with glass-panelled doors or replacing windows with French doors.

On the other hand, some homes can have too much natural light—in this case, soften the light with sheer muslin or linen curtains, or roman blinds and consider planting or other external shading.

To light the house at night, I prefer one stunning pendant rather than rows of downlights—in fact in general, only kitchens and bathrooms tend to need downlights. If one pendant doesn't give enough light, support it with table and floor lamps. Layering light in this way creates a lovely ambience.

The queen of all pendant lighting is the chandelier; if you're lucky to find a genuine antique piece, remember to have the wiring checked by an electrician (if it's too expensive to have re-wired, use drip-less candles instead of bulbs).

When entertaining, or just relaxing, there's nothing quite like the soft, ethereal beauty of candlelight. However, traditional paraffin wax candles produce a black soot that contains at least two known carcinogenic toxins, so it's much more beneficial to seek out healthy soy oil candles instead.

I do miss the lovely warm, creamy light of the old tungsten lamps but the good news is the newer compact fluros are ever evolving and getting warmer and less flickering by the day.

A Note on Hanging Pendants and Chandeliers

Pendants and chandeliers need high enough ceilings so that you can freely walk under them with plenty of room to spare. The exception is over a table or kitchen bench and in this instance the bottom of the pendant should be at least 30 in (75 cm) above the table or bench top if your ceilings are 7 ft 10.5 in (2.4 m), proportionally higher if your ceilings are higher.

Always have pendants and chandeliers installed by a qualified electrician.

The Green Clean

For a healthier and more enjoyable way to clean, follow these simple recipes.

What You Need

Pure soap

White vinegar

Baking soda

Eucalyptus oil

Tea Tree oil

Lemons

Borax

All-Purpose Surface Spray

To make your own all-purpose surface spray to clean benches, mirrors, windows, toilet seats and other surfaces, mix the following ingredients into a spray bottle.

¾ cup white vinegar

¼ cup water

20 drops eucalyptus oil

All-Purpose Surface Cream

This is a slightly more abrasive surface cleaner, which is particularly good on chrome and porcelain surfaces. Simply mix the baking soda and water together to form a paste, which you rub on and wipe off. It'll leave a lovely shine.

4 tablespoons baking soda

4 tablespoons warm water

Floor Cleaner

I love this recipe for cleaning floors. When you add the baking soda to the vinegar, it fizzes up, which is somehow very satisfying.

A bucket of hot water
½ cup vinegar
¼ cup baking soda
A few drops of tea tree oil

Disinfectant

This is a more eco-friendly disinfectant for regular household use. Borax is a natural mineral and therefore not harmful to the environment—however, it's not so gentle on the skin, so wear gloves and keep away from children.

¼ cup borax
¼ cup vinegar
Juice of ½ a lemon
Hot water

Dishwashing Powder

Commercial dishwashing powder is one of the most toxic chemicals found in the home. Use less of it by substituting half of the powder for baking soda, and using white vinegar in the rinse cycle.

Cleaning Windows

Windows come up beautifully if you wash them with hot, soapy water and then rinse them with clean hot water and vinegar.

Things to Love

A Seriously Good Sofa

A really good sofa is paramount. Don't waste money on a cheapie that'll only last a few years—buy a quality sofa and it will last you 30 years. A quality sofa should be inner-sprung, constructed with a hardwood base and made locally. For longevity, select a linen-look fabric in a neutral colour that won't date—and choose a simple, classic design.

A Hotel-Luxe Bed

Most of us probably sleep on an inner-spring mattress filled with foam and cotton or coconut fibres. However, at the very high-end of the market, mattresses are filled with cashmere, wool and silk. How gorgeous is that! To further enhance the opulence of it all, dress the bed in Italian fine linen and add an over-filled deep-diamond upholstered bedhead covered in a lush designer fabric.

Designer Wallpaper

Creating a really comfortable home is all about layering—and wallpaper literally adds another layer. The design choices are astounding and range from vividly coloured cut-velvet dogs to subtle tone-on-tone damasks. Feature wallpaper looks best on a wall that is an architectural feature in itself, so there is a natural stop and start point for the paper. If this isn't the case, paint the remaining walls in the background colour of the paper, this way it will blend seamlessly.

Curtains That Puddle

Terribly impractical, I know, as they make washing the floor quite difficult—but there's just something so gorgeously decadent in all that excess fabric! Textiles that drape well, such as silks and sheers, work particularly well. These finer fabrics gather well and look lovely on a delicate pencil pleat heading. Be as generous with the fullness as you are with the length.

Sunshine and Flowers

I think one of the prettiest sights in a home is dappled light falling into a room—perhaps created by a soft sheer curtain or external foliage. Flowers are also worth a mention. In my work as an interior stylist for magazines, I always arrive to shoots with buckets full of fresh blooms. Flowers really do make a big difference, they add life and beauty to even the simplest room.

ROOM BY ROOM
decadent decorating

Too often contemporary kitchens lack soul.
When decorating, approach the kitchen as you
would any other room in the house...

Fresh oysters w/ . . . . .

Chermoula Lamb Cutlets w/
yoghurt & mint

Semi-dried
vine tomato
pastries w/
caramelisedonion
+ basil

Asparagus,
Gruyere &
Prosciutto Tarts

Roast Carrot &
Beetroot Salad
w/ garlic & thyme

Fattoush
Salad

Chocolate
mud cup
cakes w/
strawberries

Yum!

The Kitchen

- Update a plain kitchen instantly by adding an incredible chandelier or row of vintage industrial lights. For a more organic feel, you could also try to make your own pendants from woven lobster pots or bamboo garden cloches.

- Choose timeless materials and finishes such as timber, stone or steel for cabinetry and bench tops— soften with natural fabrics such as cotton and linen. A relaxed roman blind, in cotton or linen, works particularly well in the kitchen.

- Avoid installing an overtly contemporary kitchen into an older home; it will look horribly dated in ten years (think of how many times you've walked into a home and thought, '80s kitchen' or '90s kitchen'). Select traditional finishes and classic designs.

- Transform tired, old kitchen stools with a coat of wood stain or high gloss paint and recover seats in a heavy linen (or try an eco outdoor fabric for a more easy-care option).

- Add more character to plain cabinetry doors by including moulded panels. Simply remove the doors and lightly sand before attaching the panels, then re-paint and re-hang.

- Wallpaper can add movement and colour to an otherwise neutral kitchen. Be bold by papering an entire wall, or paper behind glass-fronted cabinets for a more subtle impact. Paper is fine in the kitchen as long as it's away from wet areas—alternatively select a hardier, washable vinyl.

Opposite: When the owners first bought this property, they disliked the existing tiles, so ripped them up and diamond polished the raw concrete slab. As the structural slab wasn't designed to be polished there are subsequent imperfections, which the owners love. They chose to avoid chemicals by not having it sealed with a polyurethane coating, instead they will repolish when needed.

This compact kitchen/laundry is strikingly decorated in wallpaper. Paper, as opposed to vinyl, functions perfectly in a kitchen as long as it's kept away from the wet areas.

When installing a new kitchen in an older home, simple, classic design choices will sit most comfortably. In this kitchen, translucent roman blinds hide an unpleasant view while still allowing light to penetrate.

The Bathroom

- A freestanding bath makes the biggest statement. The old claw-foot baths are still the best as they were built to last (which is why you still see them standing around in fields and paddocks). If you're lucky enough to find one, have it re-enamelled inside and paint the outside a deep charcoal, teal or another slightly unexpected shade.

- Select lighting that you would more commonly find in other rooms; a chandelier adds instant decadence, while lamp-style wall sconces create a luxury hotel ambience.

- Mount wall sconces at eye-height on either side of the mirror for the most flattering light (overhead light will cast shadows on your face, highlighting wrinkles and worse!).

- Natural light is the most beautiful of all in a bathroom—if you don't have enough, consider adding a skylight or replacing a small window with a bigger window. If, on the other hand, you have too much natural light, soften with curtains and paint or tile the walls in a darker, moodier shade.

- Freestanding furniture creates an opulent but relaxed feel. Vintage dressers can be used in place of fitted cabinetry, just ensure all timber pieces are painted or sealed.

- Select 'real' finishes and materials, such as sealed timber, travertine and river stones wherever possible. (Timber requires some maintenance, as it needs to be re-sealed now and then, but it brings so much warmth and character to the room, it's worth it.)

- Outdoor fabric is designed to tolerate moisture and will perform well in a bathroom. It can be used for roman blinds, curtains or even shower curtains. Add a burst of colour with a bright French stripe.

- An oversized mirror will look fabulous in any sized bathroom and will double the sense of space in a small bathroom.

- Wallpaper will add instant luxe. Just remember to choose a vinyl paper, ensure the room has adequate ventilation (or the paper will eventually lift) and select a wall well away from the shower.

- Select unusual cabinet handles such as crystal-style knobs or a mismatched collection of vintage handles.

- If space permits, add a comfortable chair, for sitting and chatting to bathers. If your bathroom is too steamy for an upholstered chair, sew a terry-towelling slipcover for a timber chair.

- If possible, re-locate the toilet to a separate room—at the very least, hide it with a concealed cistern and a simple partition (and decorate with pressed tin panels or a striking patterned tile).

Eating well is one of life's greatest pleasures; and dining rooms, even in an open-plan design, should be comfortable and inviting.

The Dining Room

- If you entertain a lot, a big, comfortable table is paramount. Whether it's a beautiful old antique or a 'found' piece, if it's big and well set it'll look fabulous. (As a rough guide, each diner will need 24 in (60 cm) to sit comfortably, and you'll need to have the table at least 32 in (80 cm) away from the wall so chairs can be pulled in and out.)

- If space is tight, consider commissioning a bespoke table and specify it be only 31½–35½ in (80–90 cm) wide, rather than the more common 39¼–47 in (100–120 cm). Save even more room by teaming with a built-in banquet seat, which could also double as storage.

- Create your own 'harlequin' set of vintage chairs for next to nothing (one-off chairs are miles cheaper than sets and can be easily sourced at antique stores, charity shops and garage sales). To tie the chairs together, keep the seats at similar heights and re-paint them in the same colour.

- If you're purchasing new chairs, stick to classic designs such as a Windsor chair, Thonet bentwood or steel Tolix—these timeless designs won't date and will retain their value. Whichever chair you choose, keep in mind it needs to be comfortable—add cushions if you need to.

- In an open-plan home, a large area rug can be used to define the dining space. The rug should be big enough so that chairs can be pulled back without slipping off (however, keep in mind a rug under the dining table is a little harder to clean than bare floors).

- Chandeliers and pendants need to sit at least 30 in (75 cm) above the table. To calculate how big a chandelier should be in relation to your table; subtract 15 in (30 cm) from the width of the table.

- Antique embroidered lace tablecloths are often too small or stained in spots—cut out the good sections and sew together to create one gorgeous large tablecloth.

Opposite: Matthew Cheyne's 'Penelope' looks down over the large contemporary dining table, which has been teamed with 1950s brushed metal French chairs.

A custom bench seat and narrower-than-normal table help to save on much needed space in this compact dining area.

The Living Room

- A really good sofa is paramount. Don't waste money on a cheap one that will only last a few years—invest in a well-built piece that will last decades. A good-quality sofa should be inner-sprung, constructed with a solid timber base (preferably hardwood) and made locally. For longevity, select a heavy linen-look fabric in a neutral shade and choose a simple, classic design.

- Alternatively, be daring enough to cover your sofa in a really fabulous and unexpected colour or pattern and turn it into a real hero piece. Make sure it's a fabric you really love, as you'll need to decorate around it.

- 'Found' timber and metal furniture is perfect for the living room—and can save you a fortune on buying new. Revamp with a coat of fresh paint or a black wood wash.

- If you require additional seating, consider making up some floor cushions—especially great for movie nights and children. Remember to pre-shrink the fabric first for easy washing (see A Note on Pre-shrinking Fabric in the Fabulous Fabrics and Wonderful Wallpapers chapter).

- Storage is usually a high priority in living areas. If you opt for custom built-in cabinetry, it usually looks best in a charcoal, white or timber finish. Alternatively, for something more creative, source free-standing vintage pieces and re-purpose.

- Hang what makes you happy, whether that be a vintage ballet print, high-end artwork or a painting by your six-year-old niece. However, frame it well—everything looks better framed and behind glass. If you're hanging a collection of different-sized works, line them up at the bottom to achieve a sense of order.

- One big rug is always better than many small rugs. To define the living area in an open-plan home, place a large area rug under the coffee table and sofa (preferably, all four legs of the sofa should be on the rug; however, you can get away with just the front two).

- Rather than two matching sofas, consider one sofa paired with a couple of vintage armchairs (try wing, tub or club) in really cool fabrics—much cosier and more personalised.

- If you want your television to be discreet, mount it to a dark painted or papered wall.

- Living and television-viewing rooms don't need to be over-lit. Install dimmers on pendant lighting and ensure all lamps are well shaded to avoid glare.

Feature wallpaper works best on walls which are an
architectural feature in their own right.

A former school cupboard has been given a new lease of
life as a family's linen cupboard

A Note on Storage

If you opt for custom built-in cabinetry, use the opportunity to design the perfect storage for your household. Consider including pullout toy bins for toddlers, school bag cupboards for older children or perhaps a drinks cabinet for yourself. The more organised your home, the more relaxed you'll feel.

Deep diamond-buttoned fabric ottomans look great in the living room and can be fitted with hinged lids to store magazines and books– as can a purpose-built window seat.

And don't forget the best storage tip of all– get rid of anything you don't use or need– the less you have to put away, the better!

The Bedroom

- A big comfortable bed is a worthwhile investment so buy the best you can afford. And try linen sheeting—it's natural, beautifully tactile and the fibres soften further and grow even more lovely with wear.

- Whether to buy an ensemble or slat bed is a personal choice; slat beds work well in humid climates as they allow more air to circulate, but ensembles somehow feel more luxurious. If you do choose an ensemble, cover the base with a bespoke tailored linen bed skirt.

- Unusual bedside choices, such as metal tables, look striking, but be prepared to be seriously tidy—bedsides with drawers are much more practical. As a general rule of thumb, bedside tables should be the same height as the top of the mattress and lamps no higher than the top of the headboard.

- Wallpaper lends a sense of glamour and can be used on all walls, as a feature wall, or even on the bedhead. If you choose to do only one feature wall, make it the wall behind your bed—and paint the remaining walls in the paper's background colour.

- Install double rods (or tracks) so that you can indulge in two sets of curtains; one heavier and lined with block-out to keep out the early morning light, and one sheer to allow a softer version of the daylight in without losing privacy.

- We very rarely need strong overhead lighting in the bedroom; opt for soft, indirect light from low-wattage lamps and wall sconces instead. Have two-way switches installed, with one switch next to the bed, so you don't have to get up to turn off the lights (and also ask for all lights to be fitted with dimmers).

- As the bedroom is a space where you are likely to be barefooted, think about indulging in fine floor treatments. The tactile pleasure of plush wool carpet, or thick sheepskin rugs thrown over smooth bare floors is hard to resist.

The floors in this bedroom were a yellow-based pine, the owner had them stained in a dark hue. While they still don't quite look like hardwood floors, and will perhaps yellow up again over time, for now they look fantastic and provide an appealing contrast to the white walls and linen

Traditional timber and tin homes are notoriously lacking in storage. The wardrobe in this room is a recent addition but fits in beautifully thanks to some simple moulding. A more contemporary design would not have worked as well.

Children's Rooms

- There's something about patchwork that just works so well in a child's room. Try sourcing vintage handkerchiefs and sewing them together to create a small sheer curtain; buy wallpaper samples and attach them, patchwork-style, above the bed. You can sometimes find sample books of vintage wallpaper online. You can tear out the pages and attach them to the wall with glue, Blu-Tack or pins (if kids can't reach the pins); or make a patchwork throw out of your child's outgrown clothes.

- Stripes also work beautifully; they never date and it'll take many years for your child to outgrow them. Use masking tape (and a steady hand) to paint stripes onto a dresser; hang thickly striped wallpaper; invest in a striped wool rug; or make up striped canvas slipcovers for chairs and ottomans.

- Avoid MDF furniture where possible. Revamp solid timber pieces instead. However, always make sure any pre-loved nursery furniture complies with current safety standards.

- If you're painting the walls white, it's a good idea to choose a soft off-white rather than a stark pure white, which sometimes looks too clinical for a child's room.

- Install cotton or linen curtains, or roman blinds lined with blockout fabric to encourage longer sleep-ins and afternoon naps. Plain roman blinds can be beautifully embellished and personalised by embroidery, appliqué or a trim. Be aware of safety issues with blinds and curtains; children can get entangled in the cords.

- Customise a pendant drum light by carefully cutting away the original fabric and replacing with strips of ribbon. Tie or glue the strips on to the top frame and allow them to flutter down past the bottom frame. Always ensure the frame is large enough to keep the ribbon a safe distance away from the globe—and never fully enclose the globe, always leave the top and bottom open. (Though this is less of an issue with the new compact fluoro lamps, which don't tend to throw off much heat).

- Find and display pieces that help tell the child's story; it might be a favourite tutu from a ballet concert or a vintage tricycle, which has been passed down through the generations.

- If in doubt when decorating a child's room, opt for soft white walls and white furniture (revamped vintage pieces look superb) and team with linen and accessories in your child's favourite colours. It's a scheme that always looks good and it's incredibly easy to update.

A vintage metal child's chair and Kewpie doll.

Re-decorating for Renters

When you're renting, you may not think it's worth doing too much as it's not your house—however, keep in mind, it is your home. I've had some lovely private rental situations where the landlords/ladies did let me do little alterations around the home (such as dig a garden or paint the internal walls) and they were charming about it. However, some owners and real estate agents are more difficult, so always seek permission in writing first if you want to make any substantial changes.

Whether you are allowed to make any substantial or structural changes or not, you can certainly make the following superficial changes (just remember to have everything back to how it was when you leave).

- Update cupboard doors by replacing the handles; just remember to keep the old ones so you can pop them back on when you move out.
- Replace tired, plain light shades with more interesting ones. Keep in mind you can only do this with simple D.I.Y. batten-fixed shades. To check whether you have a D.I.Y. batten-fixed shade, try to unscrew it. If it easily unscrews with no exposed wiring, it's fine to remove and replace with a new shade. However, if this isn't the case and the shade doesn't easily unscrew, you will have to call in an electrician.
- Pack away any outdated curtains and replace with simple and affordable calico or muslin curtains. Muslin is lovely and light and makes a great sheer curtain (see How-to Simple Sheer Curtain) and calico is a more affordable alternative to linen for windows that need more coverage (see How-to Linen Curtain).
- If you have unattractive overhead cupboard doors, try removing them to create open shelving instead. You may find the cupboard carcases are a plain white and much more appealing to live with.
- Beautify nurseries and children's rooms with adorable designer removeable wall stickers. Fabric wall stickers are healthier and more eco-friendly than vinyl.
- If you'd love a linen-upholstered bedhead (see How-to) but don't want to leave holes in the wall, make a much taller bedhead that rests directly on the ground—easy to take with you and no patching up of walls.
- If you have a lot of art, consider mounting a picture rail, professional tracking system, or shelf, which will leave you with fewer holes to repair when you leave. Alternatively, attach foam pads to the backs of large pieces and gently lean them against the wall.
- Large area rugs will hide unattractive floors and, as an added benefit, will protect floors from damage. More affordable options include the natural weaves such as sisal and jute.

THE PAINTBOX

how to work with paint & colour

Colour

Inspiration

Colour is one of the most profound tools we can use in interior design. Colour inspiration can be found anywhere, but I find fashion magazines particularly helpful as not only do interior trends follow fashion trends, so you can see what will be happening in advance, but also fashion designers seem willing to push the boundaries and throw some very unexpected colours and patterns together.

White

If you love the idea of an all-white scheme, the trick is to play around with depth and introduce plenty of tonal variation. It's also easier to stick to the same school of white (see The Right White). My personal preference is to work with light, warm whites (soft whites). Cool whites, especially those that are produced by the mixing in of a little black, are more sterile to live with. White works beautifully with natural materials such as stone, timber and linen.

Going Dark

While dark walls are usually oppressive and over-powering en masse—a well-thought out feature wall can look incredible (by well-thought out, I mean a wall that has been specifically designed as a feature, perhaps an alcove in a large living area or a dividing wall between a dining and kitchen—not a random wall in a rectangular room, this generally does not look good). As with whites, the warmer shades, such as dark muddy charcoals and chocolates work best.

French Greys

Another perennial choice is French Grey—again, keep the tones warm. A warm green-grey will be much nicer to live with than a cool blue-grey. A good hint for achieving an authentic looking shade is to use natural paints. Natural paints are made with natural pigments, which are 'earthier' in appearance than synthetic pigments. These colours were originally designed with natural pigments anyway.

Difficult Colours

While some colours are complementary and always work well together, such as red and green, others are more troublesome. However, almost any colours can go together if you match the tone. So, while royal blue may not look good with mint green, muted (greyed off) blues and greens look beautiful together as do electric blue and emerald green. It's all in the tone and the intensity.

Warm, natural materials such as timber add depth to a serene white-on-white scheme. The lampshade was made by deconstructing an old shade back to its naked frame and then hand stitching on pieces of vintage linen. For details on the cushion, see Vintage Linen Detail How-to.

The Right White

With hundreds of shades available, choosing which white paint to work with can be tricky—but much easier if you have a basic understanding of how they are categorised. Broadly speaking, whites fall into three groups: neutral, cool and warm.

Neutral Whites

These are the pure whites—the 'white-whites'. A pure white will be too harsh for most home interior applications (with the exception of a very contemporary space) and better suited to art galleries and other commercial buildings. The whites in most homes are, in fact, off-whites.

Cool Whites

Cool whites are technically off-whites as they have undertones of blue, green, grey or black.

Cool whites are crisp, fresh and very contemporary and work well with contemporary architecture—the cool hues echoed in man-made materials such as stainless steel and glass.

The cool tints are literally cooling, making these shades perfect for homes that receive too much sun. In this instance, it's best to choose a deeper shade of cool white to help soften any potential glare.

Warm Whites

Warm, creamy whites, are also technically off-whites as they have undertones of red, brown or yellow.

Warm whites have a traditional feel to them and suit older-style homes perfectly. They inject warmth and intimacy into a room and work well with natural textures like timber.

Though warm whites will literally warm up a sun-deprived home—choose the lightest shades possible to add more light.

Painting Tips for White

White looks best when it's layered and there's a simple way to do this—use the same white on walls, skirtings and ceilings, but in different strengths and gloss levels:

- Use full strength on the walls, half strength on the skirtings and quarter on the ceiling.

- Use low-sheen acrylic on the walls, high gloss on the skirtings and a flat finish on the ceiling.

Gently manipulating the same shade of white in this way will create subtle shading and variation, which prevents the room from looking flat.

Order for Painting an Entire Room

1. Cornices and ceilings– first coat

2. Walls– first coat

3. Cornices and ceilings– final coat

4. Skirtings, architraves and doors– first coat

5. Walls– final coat

6. Skirtings, architraves and doors– final coat

Tips for Painting Walls

- Buy special removable masking tape from a paint shop— regular masking tape can be hard to remove and it's a little disheartening if your paint work ends up being messed up in the process!

- Buy good-quality brushes. Cheaper brushes tend to lose more bristles— not a good look on your walls.

- Dip no more than a third of the brush into the paint at a time, gently wipe or tap excess paint back into the tin.

- 'Cutting in' with the brush before using the roller, gives the roller a little edge to work within, which prevents you accidentally painting the skirtings, etc.

- When using the roller, keep the edges wet to avoid overlap marks.

Experiment with your chosen paint colour by tinting, toning or shading.

- To tint, add white

- To tone, add grey

- To shade, add black (or brown)

Remember, if you tint, tone or shade almost any mismatched bunch of colours to the same degree, they will suddenly sit together in perfect harmony

Exterior House Colours

When selecting exterior house colours, avoid bright hues, as they have the tendency to look kitsch. The classic colours work best; try charcoals, taupes, biscuits, creams and off-whites. Avoid pure white, which looks too harsh. Two or three colours are more than enough; any more will look too busy.

French washed walls

A Note on Paint Types

Traditionally there were two basic paint types: acrylic (or water-based) paints and enamel (or oil-based) paints. However, due to the high toxicity of enamel paint, new water-based enamels have entered the market. Though some argue they're not quite as glossy and hardwearing as traditional oil-based enamels, water-based enamels are much less toxic and, therefore, a much better choice.

A Note on Cleaning Up

If you've been painting with water-based paints, you can rinse brushes, rollers and trays in the sink; if you've used oil-based paints, you will have to rinse off in turps.

If you have leftover paint, it must be thrown into the bin, rather than down the drain. However, as most councils won't allow you to throw liquid paint into your bin, you'll have to solidify it first. The easiest way to do this is by mixing in some kitty litter or sand.

How to

Milk Paint

Milk paint is 100 per cent natural, non-toxic and biodegradable. It is one of the safest paints available (which makes it perfect for nurseries and children's rooms)—and with no 'paint' smell, it is a joy to use.

It is also possibly the world's oldest paint. Cave drawings and paintings, at least 8000 years old, have been found coloured in a simple form of milk paint made from milk, lime and earth pigment. For thousands of years, the recipe for milk paint remained relatively unchanged and the ingredients were readily available.

However, in the 1860s the invention of the metal paint can saw the beginning of the commercial paint industry. As milk paint, like all milk products, spoils fairly rapidly and must be made as needed rather than pre-mixed, it was oil-based paint (made with highly poisonous additives) that was mass-produced for the new industry.

Though many of the more dangerous chemicals have since been banned from synthetic paint, and paint companies are developing an increasing number of paints with lower VOCs (volatile organic compounds), it is still predominantly the natural paints, such as milk paint, which have no VOCs.

Milk paint can be made from scratch using casein powder (milk protein), pigment powder and water. However, for convenience it is easier to buy it commercially.

Either way, the paint is quite gorgeous to work with. You simply whisk the powder with water until it forms a creamy batter and leave to stand until it thickens a little. It will continue to thicken as you paint but, once dry, the finish is consistent and very smooth and can be sealed with natural beeswax.

Milk paint is velvety soft, both in colour and texture—and the end result is reminiscent of the traditional lime-washed walls seen in the likes of France and Italy.

MIX AND USE MILK PAINT

Commercial milk paint comes as a powder that you mix up with water as you go. How much paint you mix up at a time comes down to a little guesswork, but I usually start with around three cups of powder. (If you have any mixture left over, you can cover it in plastic wrap and keep it in the fridge for up to 24 hours.)

WHAT YOU NEED

A bag of milk paint

2 bowls

A wooden spoon or whisk

A stocking or piece of muslin to strain with

A good-quality brush

Beeswax or clear sealer to seal

METHOD

1. Pour the powder into a bowl and mix with enough water to form a 'pancake batter' consistency. Whisk well to get all the lumps out.

2. Leave to thicken for 10 minutes.

3. Strain the mixture through a stocking into a second bowl (though as I didn't have any stockings, I used one of my daughter's old ballet tights, or you could use a piece of muslin).

4. You're now ready to paint. The mixture will continue to thicken as you work—and at times it will feel as if you are painting with yoghurt rather than milk—but once dry, the finish is consistent and very smooth.

5. Once the first coat is dry, sand lightly before applying the second coat.

6. Seal with natural beeswax or an all-purpose clear sealer.

PAINT INTERIOR WALLS

If previously painted walls are in good condition—and aren't too high—they're very simple to re-paint.

WHAT YOU NEED

Sugar soap

Cloth

Drop sheets

Masking tape

Undercoat (optional)

Low-sheen acrylic paint

Paint brush

Roller and roller tray

METHOD

1. Clean walls thoroughly with sugar soap and a cloth and allow them to dry.

2. Drag furniture into the middle of the room and cover with drop sheets, apply masking tape to light fittings, power outlets and along skirtings and trims, and place more drop sheets on the ground.

3. Apply one coat of undercoat to seal and prime walls (in much the same way as you might apply a primer to your face before applying foundation). This step must be taken if walls are raw or in poor condition—however, you can skip this step if the walls are already painted AND are in perfect condition.

4. Apply the first coat of paint. Use a paintbrush to cut in along the edges, cornices and skirtings—use the roller to fill in the main part of the wall.

5. Allow the first coat to dry before applying the second coat.

FRENCH WASH WALLS

French washing is a very old, traditional technique, which adds subtle movement and a soft beauty to walls. This is a two-person project, both simple and fun.

For the best results, start in one spot and keep moving in one direction around the whole room until you're back at the beginning. You need to work fairly fast as the wash is quite runny.

WHAT YOU NEED

Sugar soap

Cloth

Low-sheen acrylic (base coat)

French wash

A large muslin cloth

Brush

METHOD

1. Clean and prepare wall thoroughly with sugar soap and a cloth and allow them to dry.

2. Apply two coats of the low-sheen acrylic and allow to dry.

3. Apply the French wash. This needs two people. The first person applies the French wash with a brush, using messy, multi-directional strokes (rather than nice up-and-down strokes). The second person follows with a muslin cloth, scrunched into a messy bundle, using it to gently dab the walls.

2.

PORTER'S ORIGINAL

Muslin cloth

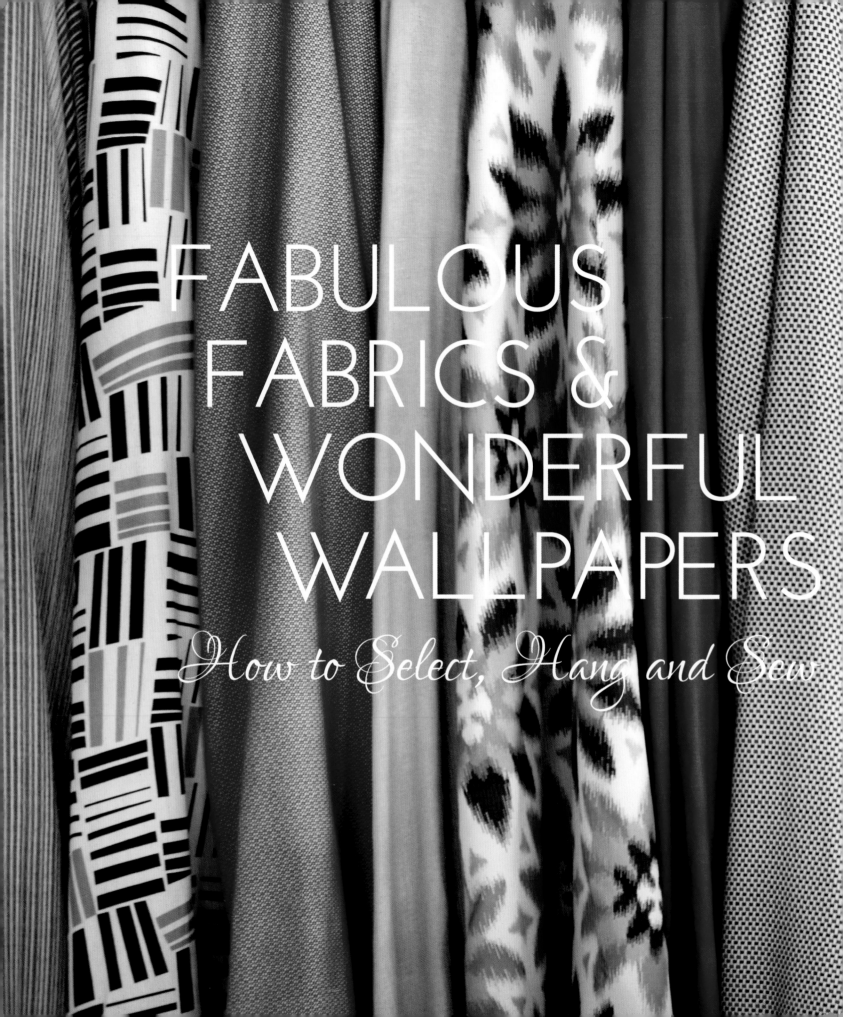

FABULOUS FABRICS & WONDERFUL WALLPAPERS

How to Select, Hang and Sew

Selecting Fabrics

Fabric Categories

Broadly speaking, interior fabric falls into four categories; sheer, drapery, upholstery and outdoor. With the exception of sheer, all can be used for cushioning—however, most drapery fabrics are not hardy enough for upholstery projects and heavier upholstery fabrics won't drape well—so it's best to stick to the correct categories.

Natural vs Synthetic

Tactically and aesthetically, most people enjoy naturals over synthetics. My utopian home would have thick linen sofas, organic cotton sheets and oversized silk curtains puddling onto the floor. However, natural fabrics do have their downfalls. They have a tendency to crease, fade and stain (not that that's necessarily a bad thing; a crushed linen curtain or a faded vintage silk cushion has a certain sensual appeal).

If you have pets or young children and need a hardier textile, 100 per cent synthetics are inherently stain resistant and might be a more affordable and practical choice on sofas and the like. The trick is to select a synthetic with a linen-look weave rather than one that looks too artificial.

Outdoor Fabrics

Natural fabrics have a tendency to fade and break down in the sun, so for longevity use specifically designed outdoor fabric in outside areas. Some of the hardier designer outdoor fabrics are made from the likes of olefin and they're easy to live with, as they're soft to the touch yet extremely durable. The downside is the production of these fabrics is not very eco-friendly. For a greener range try Bella-Dura (www.bella-dura.com).

Eco Choices

Though it's quite hard to find eco outdoor fabric, luckily there are plenty of options when it comes to interior textiles. Most green designers will print with water-based inks on an organic base cloth. Some even use mechanical, rather than the more common chemical, processes such as pressing and heating to achieve specific finishes. Try O Eco Textiles (www.oecotextiles.com), Mod Green Pod (www.modgreenpod.com) and Cloth Fabric (www.clothfabric.com).

Vintage and Remnant

If you'd like to create something truly unique, consider sourcing vintage and remnant fabrics. You may be limited by fabric lengths, however smaller pieces can always be sewn together to create interesting contemporary patchwork tablecloths, cushions or quilts. You'll also have the added satisfaction of not consuming more new product (for further inspiration watch 'Story of Stuff' on YouTube).

Photo on following page: Double curtains, incorporating one sheer and one heavier lined curtain, will allow you to better control the levels of privacy, heat and light desired. Though the shade appears to be in a matching fabric at first glance, it isn't.

Which Window Treatment?

Roller Blinds

Roller blinds are not perhaps the most inspired choice, aesthetically speaking, however they're cheap and practical. While many of us remember the unattractive plastic-look blinds of the past, today's fabric choices are much improved and include synthetics that closely resemble linens and self-patterned 'cut out' designs. Use translucent blind fabrics if you want to allow in the daylight but wish to retain privacy (however, you will lose some privacy at night once you turn an inside light on) and full blockout blinds if you require better insulation and full day and night privacy. Generally speaking, roller blinds are best suited to more contemporary homes and commercial buildings.

Roman Blinds

Roman blinds are extremely versatile as they can be made with almost any fabric (within reason—for example, a very heavy fabric will not stack well) and can be designed to look very relaxed (think of a simple Swedish-style, unlined cotton roman) or more high-end (imagine a very tailored, linen blind in a designer fabric). The price of roman blinds is dependent on the fabric you choose, however they're generally quite a bit cheaper than curtains as they require less fabric to make. They work particularly well on higher windows, such as those above a bed, where full-length curtains aren't suitable. Keep in mind most light penetrates through the top portion of your window, so if you want to retain as much light as possible (or perhaps a view) mount the blinds 8 in (20 cm) or so above the architrave.

Curtains

Curtains have made a big comeback in recent years and really have the ability to 'dress' a room. Some still remember the curtains of their childhood and can't see them as desirable but it's all in the fabric. As a seventies kid, I remember a plethora of polyester. However, the trick is to use natural fabrics (or at least natural-looking fabrics) and the right design. For a relaxed style, try a simple unlined linen (see Unlined Linen Curtain how-to). For a more luxurious feel, try hotel-style double curtains, a light sheer under a heavier lined curtain. Mount tracks 6 to 8 in (15 to 20 cm) above the top architrave (if possible) to create a greater sense of height—and 8 to 11¾ in (20 to 30 cm) past each side so the fabric has room to stack back without impeding light or view. Regardless of where the window stops, curtains tend to look best if they fall to the floor.

Lining and Interlining

If you need to protect more delicate fabrics from the sun, simply line them with anything from simple cotton to a full blockout, depending on how much protection they'll need. Lining will also help with noise suppression and protect against heat loss/gain. You can take this one step further by adding interlining. Interlining is a soft, fleecy fabric that is added between the main fabric and the lining, which intensifies the insulation properties. It also adds a greater sense of luxury as the curtain will be heavier and drape more beautifully (however, interlining does make curtains harder to wash and isn't particularly suited to damp or humid climates). And just a little 'healthy home' thought—if you need full blockout curtains but are reluctant to use plastic-style backings (which off-gas nasties), try cotton lining with natural interlining instead.

Plantation Shutters and Venetians

Though they don't offer the insulation properties of lined curtains and romans, white plantation shutters have a fresh, summery appeal and can work very well in warmer climates, allowing easy manipulation of light and air-flow. However, be aware that they aren't particularly suited to bedrooms, as they will almost always let in slithers of morning light. Their other downfall is they're quite expensive. However, if you're on a budget you could try ordering venetian blinds with extra wide (approximately 3 in/8 cm) blades instead—this will give a similar appearance at a fraction of the price.

Vintage embroidered tablecloths make light, pretty curtains. This one, bought for a few dollars at a charity store, is secured very simply by a couple of nails hidden in the top window frame.

A Note on Pre-Shrinking Fabric

It's a superb idea to make cushion covers, slipcovers, curtains and throws out of washable fabrics such as cotton and linen—however, as these fabrics will shrink by about three per cent after their first wash—you really need to wash them before you start sewing.

Simply soak the fabric in a tub of hot water for an hour or so—and then gently squeeze out the excess water before hanging out to dry (be careful to hang larger, heavier pieces over a couple of lines to prevent it from becoming misshapen).

Iron on the wrong side while still slightly damp.

How to

ENVELOPE CUSHION

The measurements given are for 18 x 18 in (45 x 45 cm) cushions (a fairly regular-sized throw cushion) and they allow for a 6 in (15 cm) overlap—however, you can adjust as desired to make different-sized cushions.

WHAT YOU NEED

Half a metre of fabric

Thread

Tape measure, scissors and pins

METHOD

1. Cut out a piece of fabric 19 x 19 in (47 x 47cm) for the front of the cushion and two pieces, 16 x 19in (39.5 x 47cm) and 10 x 19in (24.5 x 47cm) for the back (one piece is bigger to allow for the opening to overlap).

2. Along one 19 in (47 cm) edge of each back piece; iron and sew a ¼ in (1cm) seam.

3. Lay the back pieces on top of the front piece—right sides together with the back seams overlapping in the middle.

4. Pin and sew all the way around the edge of the cushion. Turn out.

ENVELOPE CUSHION, WITH A FLANGE

This is a gorgeous variation of the basic machine-sewn envelope cushion we've made on the previous page. You simply add an extra 2½ in (6 cm) of material the entire way around the cushion to create the flange.

WHAT YOU NEED

24 in (60 cm) of fabric

Thread

Tape measure, scissors and pins

METHOD

1. Cut out a piece of fabric 23⅓ x 23⅓ in (59 x 59 cm) for the front of the cushion. And two pieces, 18 x 23⅓ in (45.5 x 59cm) and 12 x 23⅓ in (30.5 x 59 cm) for the back.

2. Along one 23⅓ in (59vcm) edge of each back piece iron and sew a ¼ in (1cm) seam.

3. Lay the back pieces on top of the front piece—right sides together with the back seams overlapping in the middle.

4. Pin and sew around the edge of the cushion. Turn right side out.

5. On the right side—pin and sew a second seam, 2½ in (6 cm) in from the edge, to create the flange.

ENVELOPE CUSHION, WITH PIPING

In this variation, the process and measurements are very similar to the machine-sewn envelope cushion, except you attach piping to the front panel of the cushion before you sew the front and backs together.

WHAT YOU NEED

Half a metre of fabric

6.56 ft (2 m) of piping

Thread

Tape measure, scissors and pins

METHOD

1. Cut out a piece of fabric 18½ x 18½ in (47 x 47 cm) for the front of the cushion. And two pieces, 15½ x 18½ in (39.5 x 47 cm) and 9½ x 18½in (24.5 x 47cm) for the back.

2. Along one 18½ in (47 cm) edge of each back piece; iron and sew a ¼ in (1 cm) seam.

3. Pin the piping onto the front piece of fabric. You will have to carefully snip the piping four or five times to allow it to turn around the corners. Use the piping foot on your machine to sew the piping on.

4. Lay the front fabric on top of the back pieces, right sides together, and pin carefully. Use your piping foot again to sew the front and back pieces together. Sew from the front so you can follow the line of stitching. Turn out.

SIMPLE SHEER CURTAIN

A simple sheer curtain helps to diffuse bright sunlight without completely blocking breezes or a view.

WHAT YOU NEED

Sheer fabric

Spring clips with rings (available from sewing shops)

Thread

Tape measure, scissors and pins

METHOD

1. Measure your window from the rod to the floor. This is your drop; add 8½ in (22cm) for hemming and seams. The width of your fabric needs to be wider than your window (twice as wide is good if you can manage it).

2. Pin and sew a ¼ in (1 cm) seam around the entire piece of fabric.

3. Turn over the top by 4 in (10 cm) and hem.

4. Turn over the bottom by 4 in (10 cm) and hem.

5. Attach to rod with the spring clips.

UNLINED LINEN CURTAIN

If I need very elegant fully-lined curtains, I always have them professionally made—generally with a pencil-pleat heading and hung on a rod with gliders, so that they open and close beautifully.

However, for a more relaxed style, these unlined linen curtains are perfect—and so easy to make

WHAT YOU NEED

Linen

Thread

Tape measure, scissors and pins

METHOD

1. Pin and sew a ¼ in (1 cm) seam around all edges

2. Turn over the top by 4 in (10 cm) and hem.

3. Pin and sew a 2 in (5 cm) seam running parallel to the hem. (Check your rod is narrow enough to fit through a 2 in (5 cm) hem, or adjust the seam size accordingly).

4. Turn over the bottom by 4 in (10 cm) and hem.

2 in / 5 cm

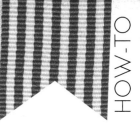

SILK THROW

WHAT YOU NEED

13 f (4 m) of silk (approximately 55 in (140 cm) wide)

6½ f (2 metres) of wadding (cut to the same width as the silk)

Silk thread

Scissors, pins, needle

Sewing machine

METHOD

1. Cut two pieces of silk, 6½ f (2 m) x width of fabric.

2. Layer the two pieces of silk on top of one another—and then layer the piece of wadding on top.

3. Pin and sew around three edges—leaving one narrow edge open.

4. Turn right side out (as you would with a doona cover). The wadding layer should now be sandwiched between the two pieces of silk.

5. Turn under the raw edges of the open end—and machine stitch across the top to close.

6. Measure and pin 4 in (10 cm) rows across the width of the throw. Hand-sew the layers together using a simple running stitch.

A Note on Wadding

Wadding is the soft layer of padding sewn into quilts to keep them warm and comfy. We used bamboo wadding for this project, but you can also find cotton, wool or polyester wadding. It's sold either buy the metre or in pieces, and it's available from fabric and quilting stores.

After

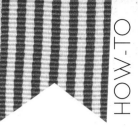

VINTAGE LINEN DETAIL

Vintage handmade hankies and napkins can be sewn onto fresh white linen to create beautifully detailed and interesting pieces. I've found charity stores are the best places to source vintage pieces, and they don't cost much at all. This is a very relaxing and easy project to do.

WHAT YOU NEED

A selection of white vintage cotton and
    linen hankies and napkins
White pillowcase or sheet
White cotton and a needle

METHOD

1. Simply place the hankies onto the linen as you desire; pin into place, and hand-sew. Use small neat stiches to go around the edge of each piece and then anchor by sewing a running stitch across the middle if needed (to stop the piece billowing out from the linen).

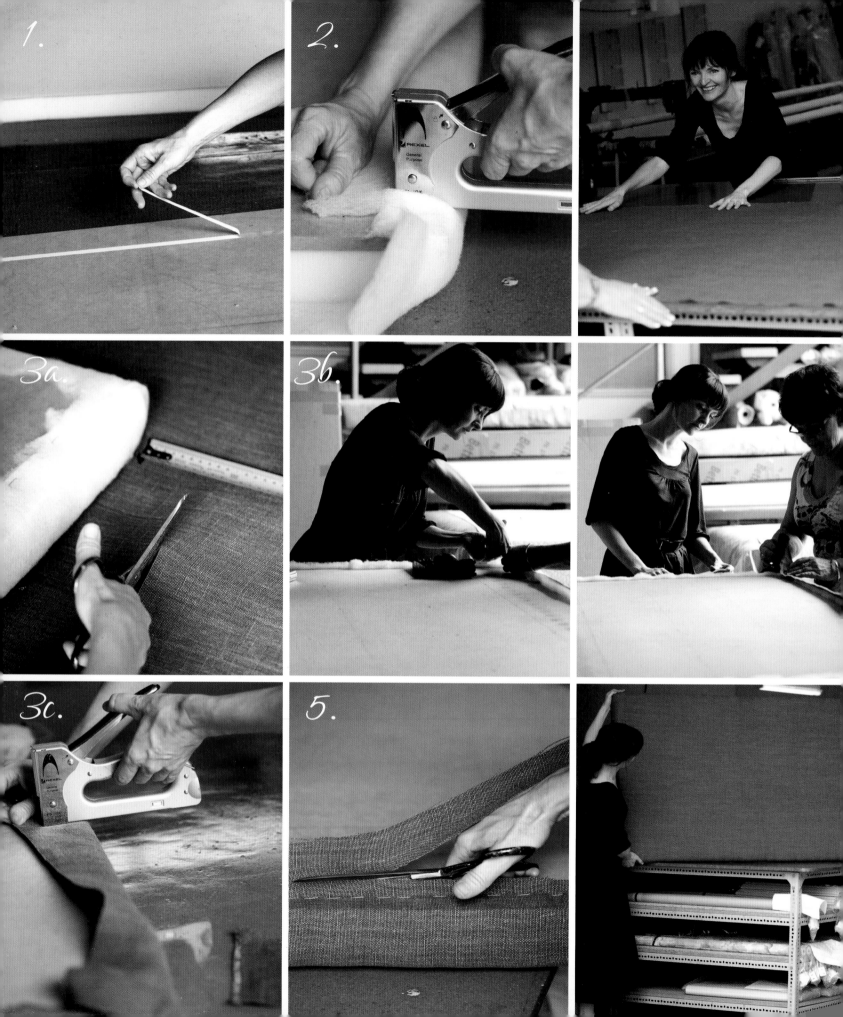

1.

2.

3a.

3b.

3c.

5.

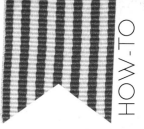

UPHOLSTERED LINEN BEDHEAD

This is surprisingly easy and quite enjoyable to make. The trick is to use a very lightweight upholstery fabric, perhaps a linen or linen/cotton blend, as anything heavier is too hard to get neat at the corners.

Also, it's easiest to work on a nice big table if you can.

MOUNTING THE HEADBOARD

Mount your headboard onto the wall using keyhole brackets and screws (available from your local hardware store). You'll need to fix them into your wall studs—if you can't find the wall studs, you'll need to buy hollow wall anchors as well.

WHAT YOU NEED

MDF board, 16 x 9 m (52½ x 29½ ft)
(Ask your local hardware store if they can cut to size—opt for EO MDF if possible. Only a few dollars more and miles healthier.)

2 in (5 cm) thick foam, 6 x 9 m (52½ x 29½ ft) (Your local foam store may be able to cut foam to size on the spot.)

Wadding, 6½ ft (2 m) (available from fabric stores)

Fabric, 6½ ft (2 m)

Double-sided tape

Staple gun

METHOD

1. Attach the foam to the MDF board with double-sided tape.

2. Lay the board, foam side down, on to the wadding. Wrap the wadding firmly around the board and staple to the back. It's easiest to start with a staple to the middle of each edge and each corner, and then go back around adding more staples. If the wadding is too bulky in the corners, trim with scissors. Trim any other excess wadding.

3. Repeat this process with the fabric.

BUTTONED BEDHEAD

A deep diamond-buttoned bedhead is the ultimate in luxury. It's not really a home project as it takes years to perfect the skill required for true diamond-buttoning.

However, with the kind help of Denise Kennedy, a soft furnishings expert and owner of Curtain Elegance, we've come up with a simple version, which mimics the real thing.

WHAT YOU NEED

Drill

Buttoning kit (12 buttons)

Left-over fabric from your bedhead

Darning needle, cord

METHOD

1. Make your bedhead as per the instructions on the previous page, except drill twelve evenly spaced holes into the MDF board before you start.

2. Cover your buttons as per the instructions on the pack.

3. Attach the buttons with the darning needle and cord. Start at the back of each pre-cut hole and push the threaded darning needle through to sew on the button, tie off and then staple at the back.

1.

3a.

3b.

3c.

3d.

3e.

Wallpaper

I love that the golden years of wallpaper were in the roaring 20s—for no other reason than it's an era I adore—and I am thrilled wallpaper is back in vogue. Papering a room adds instant opulence. Three rolls of Osborne and Little and a plain little powder room becomes something else entirely.

Wallpapers are no longer made only from paper; they are now also made from vinyl, bamboo, cotton, foil and numerous other materials. Though I still consider papers the prettiest, vinyls are excellent for areas that receive more wear and tear as they are hardier and washable (though their plastic coating does make them less eco-friendly), while grass-weaves work perfectly in natural-style interiors.

Hanging wallpaper well is an art form, and with a roll of designer papers costing quite a lot, I almost always recommend using a professional (the only exception being if it's a very small and simple wall—and you use one of the newer non-woven wallpapers which require you to paste the wall not the paper—much easier! See Hang Non-woven Wallpaper how-to for details).

Playing with Pattern

Once you find a piece of fabric or wallpaper you absolutely love, be daring enough to decorate around it. Select one of the neutral colours in the design to use as the restful colour in the room. Use this neutral colour on painted walls or perhaps the carpet. Select the most brilliant colour in the pattern to use as your accent colour. Use this colour in art, accessories and soft furnishings.

Eyes need places to rest, so it is important to have clear spaces between patterned objects. Therefore, as a general rule, look at the main elements of the room and balance the patterned with the plain. For example, if the walls are patterned keep the floors plain.

To successfully group different patterns together, simply establish a theme based on colour, texture or design. This works particularly well when different but complimentary fabrics are used in close proximity to one another, as happens commonly with cushions.

HANG NON-WOVEN WALLPAPER

Wallpapers made from traditional woven paper, vinyl and grasses are quite tricky to hang—the newer non-woven fabrics are much easier, as you paste the wall rather than the paper.

Start with a simple, straightforward wall with no obstacles (perhaps a feature wall in a bedroom—do not start with a bathroom as going around a toilet is tricky!).

Wallpaper is generally sold in rolls that are 21 in (53 cm) wide and 33 ft (10 m) long. An average wall will need two to three rolls of paper (a good tip is to check the batch numbers on the rolls, as the colours can differ quite substantially between batches).

The other great thing about non-woven wallpapers is they're dry-strippable—which makes them very easy to remove or replace when the time comes.

WHAT YOU NEED

Wallboard sealer

Sandpaper

Wallpaper size (available from wallpaper stores, its purpose is help prepare the walls)

Wallpaper

Wallpaper paste

Scissors

Roller

Straight edge spreader (a plastic tool to help smooth the paper)

Rag

Sharp knife (or Stanley knife)

Ruler (preferably with a handle to make cutting easier)

METHOD

1. Prepare the surface. If it's a new build with bare gyprock walls, seal the surface with a wallboard sealer. If the walls are painted with an acrylic paint, simply sand lightly.

2. Apply a coat of size to the wall. (Size is available from wallpaper stores and some hardware stores. Its purpose is to even up the porosity of the wall—it also gives a little bit of slip, allowing you to more easily slide the wallpaper sideways to line up patterns.)

3. Cut the wallpaper to length, allowing for overlap on both the top and bottom.

A once white, empty stairwell void is completely transformed by two rolls of wallpaper and a reading chair.

4. Apply the paste to the wall with a roller, cut in with a brush where required (if you accidently get some glue on the cornice or ceiling, don't worry, just wipe it off with a rag after you've trimmed the paper).

5. Hang the wallpaper from the top to the bottom of the wall—smoothing the paper over with a straight edge spreader as you go.

6. Trim paper along the top and bottom with a thin, sharp knife and a ruler (a ruler with a handle is easier—the ruler needs to be longer than the width of the wallpaper).

7. Repeat until the wall is done.

Before commercial wallpaper glues were readily available, wallpaper hangers used to make their own glue with flour and water. This used to work perfectly well in England, but when they tried it in warmer climates, cockroaches kept eating through the paper to get to the flour!

FOUND FURNITURE

How to restore and adore

A vintage deep-buttoned tub chair is given a new lease
of life thanks to the expert craftsmanship of Steven
Williams, whose family has owned and operated Parry

Finding and Fixing

Avoid mundane mass-produced MDF furniture and source quality old pieces instead, which you can revamp with fresh fabric, stain and paint. You'll not only end up with more interesting and eclectic pieces, but also pieces with more soul.

The best places to source affordable vintage furniture are garage sales, charity shops and by the roadside. Don't look at the tatty old fabric or a bad paint job; look at the shape and structure. You must love the shape from the beginning, as that won't change. The structure must be sound, or it could prove too difficult and costly to fix.

Don't rush in and paint a piece until you find out what it is first. If it's a genuine antique, you could severely depreciate its value if you don't restore it correctly.

If you have an everyday piece, be as daring as you like with your choices—you can't ruin it (and even if everything goes horribly wrong, you can always start again).

Restoring Antique Pieces

Andrew Baxter, from Baxter's Antique Restorations, has been restoring antiques for over 30 years. He advises that each piece must be individually assessed to determine the correct method of restoration required—but generally, restoration falls into one of the following four categories:

Revive and Wax

This method is for pieces that are in good condition, but just need a clean and polish. It achieves the same result as stripping and polishing, but is much faster and easier to do. (The vintage frame on page 140 took us one hour; it would have taken a day to strip and stain.) Use a good-quality commercially used reviver and wax.

Spot Strip

If only part of the piece is damaged, such as the top of a desk, Andrew will restore that section fully and then revive and wax the remainder. This is obviously less costly and quicker than restoring the entire piece.

Shellac and Wax

A shellac and wax is the quick version of a full restoration. It won't quite achieve the same full depth and body in the finish, but it will nicely freshen up the polish. Wash the old shellac or varnish off with stripper and then methylated spirits. Lightly sand before applying two new coats of shellac. Protect the finish with two coats of wax.

Full Restoration

For pieces that have been badly neglected and/or exposed to the elements a full restoration may be required. Strip, sand and prepare the piece for finishing by repairing any minor damage, filling any small holes and finishing with a product of your choice.

How to

VINTAGE FRAME (REVIVE AND WAX)

This beautiful 1920s frame features exquisite hand-stamped details—it was picked up at a charity shop. As it was structurally sound, it only needed to be revived and waxed.

WHAT YOU NEED

Small craft knife

Furniture reviver

Fine-grade (0000) steel wool

Soft cloths

Toothbrush

Furniture wax

Gloves

METHOD

1. Use a small craft or Stanley knife to gently scrape off any lumps of dirt (or more likely, spider poo!). Be very careful not to cut through the finish.

2. Apply the reviver with the fine-grade steel wool. It's important to follow the grain so you don't scratch the timber—and keep your strokes long and even. Use the reviver sparingly, and wipe off any excess as you go with a soft cloth.

3. Go over with a toothbrush, working in a circular motion to get into any intricately carved or moulded areas. Wipe off excess reviver.

4. Apply the wax sparingly with the steel wool (the more you put on the more you'll have to take off). Wear gloves to protect your hands and to prevent your nails being stained with black.

5. Leave to dry for approximately 10 minutes.

6. Burnish off with a soft clean rag (an old t-shirt is perfect).

before

1.

3.

4.

DIRECTIONS FOR USE

5.

6.

After

A Note on Burnishing

Burnishing just means to polish—the idea is to rub quite fast so that the wax heats up and softens as you work. This process can be repeated up to half a dozen times or until you're happy with the result. Allow the wax to dry for around an hour between coats.

before

2.

3.

4.

CARD FILE DRAWERS (REVIVE AND WAX)

I found this English oak card file drawer at my local charity shop. It had originally been used to file cards at a public library.

Card file drawers usually have slat bottoms, so small objects fall through. To rectify this, simply cut out a piece of plywood and lay it inside the drawer (I just used a piece of thick cardboard and some scissors—even easier!).

Though the finish wasn't perfect I liked its slightly worn appearance, so, like the frame, it only received a quick revive and wax. However, I did want to change the plastic knobs for metal handles (big enough to cover the original nameplate marks).

WHAT YOU NEED

Ruler

Bradawl

Drill and drill bits

Screwdriver

New handles to replace the original

METHOD

1. Remove the old knobs.

2. Use a ruler to check the new handles are centred, and mark with a bradawl (a small tool used to punch through, or in this case mark, timber, leather and other materials).

3. Use a hand or cordless drill to drill the required holes.

4. Screw on your handles (if the screws are a little hard to get in, coat them with a little soap or candle wax).

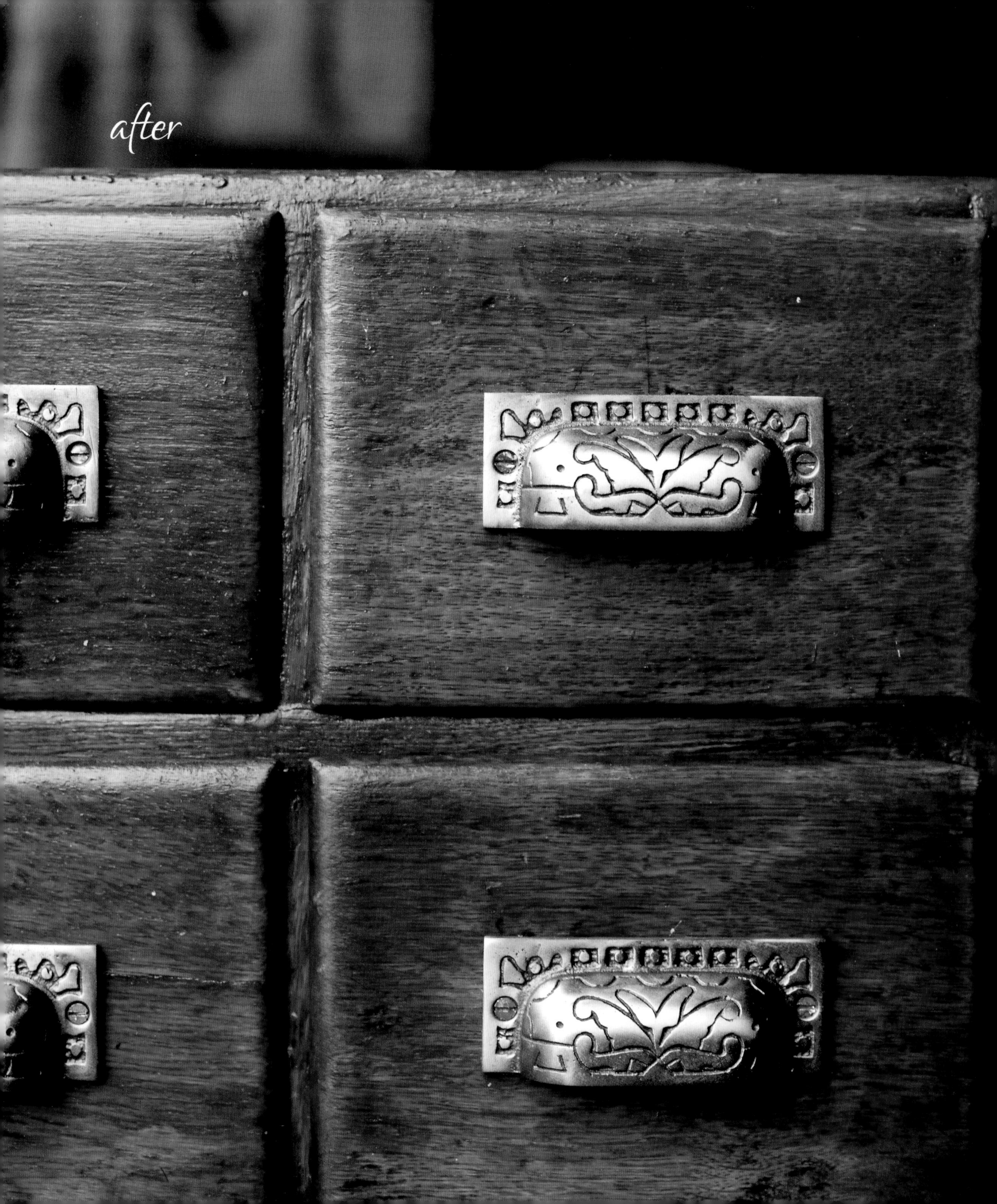
after

A Note on Painting Antiques

As beautiful as old timber is, sometimes the dark colours can be too heavy for certain rooms. If you want to paint an antique piece without devaluing it, the trick is to leave the old finish on to protect the wood— and use an oil-based enamel.

The reason for using an oil-based enamel is that it is easy to chemically strip, should you ever want to restore the piece later— whereas water-based paints need to be sanded, which can be detrimental to delicate moldings.

The bad news is oil-based enamels are pretty toxic; however, if you think it's worth preserving the original finish on an antique piece, here's how to do it.

Clean the piece with turpentine and steel wool. Wipe over with a damp cloth to remove any excess and allow to dry. Gently sand with a fine sandpaper— be careful to go with the grain so you don't scratch the finish. Apply two coats of enamel paint.

EUROPEAN BEDSIDE (SHELLAC AND WAX)

Found at a local garage sale, this bedside cabinet was originally from Europe and made from a fruit tree. The plug style knob and rustic finish made it look decidedly 'country'—but it just needed a dark stain and new crystal-style knob to dress it up.

Look for enviromentally friendly, plant-based, non-toxic, polyurethane-free wood stains.

WHAT YOU NEED

Fine hand saw

Screwdriver

Chemical stripper, gloves and safety
    glasses

Methylated spirits

Steel wool (00 and 0000 grade)

Sandpaper (150- 240- and 400-grit)

Dark wood stain (we used walnut)

Shellac

Paintbrush

Furniture wax

Bradawl, drill and drill bits

New crystal-style knob

METHOD

1. Use a hand saw to remove the wooden knob.

2. Use a screwdriver to remove fixtures from cabinet (hinges and catch) so that the cabinet door comes away.

3. Chemically strip the bedside cabinet carefully, following the manufacturer's instructions. Safety is paramount when using chemical strippers—wear industrial-strength rubber gloves, safety glasses and work in a well-ventilated area.

4. Neutralise paint stripper by washing off with methylated spirits and 00 steel wool, ensuring that you wipe off residue (methylated spirits will also evaporate fast and dry the timber, so you'll be able to work on your piece again straight away).

5. Lightly sand timber surfaces, first with 150-grit sandpaper, then with a finer 240-grit sandpaper to end with a smooth finish. (Always sand with the grain—if you sand against the grain scratches will show through after the finish is applied.)

before

1.

3.

6.

7.

9a

9b

9c.

10

after

6. Apply stain evenly with a clean rag and allow to dry.

7. Apply a fine coat of shellac with a paintbrush, enabling it to dry and recoat if necessary, cutting back between coats with 400-grade sandpaper.

8. Cut back shellac finish with 0000 grade steel wool so it has an even dull appearance, and then finish it off with the wax.

9. Use a pencil to mark where the new crystal-style knob is to go. Spike the surface with a bradawl, this ensures the drill bit will not drift when starting to drill your hole. Drill your hole and then screw your new knob into position

10. Reattach the door to the bedside.

ANTIQUE 1920S CARVER (FULL RESTORATION)

This gorgeous old boy was found under a house and it was absolutely covered in 20 years' worth of dust. Under all the dirt and grime though, was a beautiful solid maple chair with a walnut-veneered back.

Unfortunately, as it had been exposed to the weather, the finish was damaged and the chair needed to be fully restored. Andrew and one of his tradesmen, Michael, were kind enough to take on this job (it's not for the faint-hearted).

WHAT YOU NEED

Furniture Reviver
Chemical stripper, rubber gloves and
   safety glasses
Methylated spirits
Sandpaper (150-, 240- and 400-grit)
Wood stop (putty) in colour to match stain
Wood stain in colour of your choice
Soft cloths
00 and 0000 grade steel wool
Shellac
Paintbrush
Furniture wax

METHOD

1. Try and revive—hopefully that will leave you with a smooth and clean finish. If that method doesn't work and the surface is still rough or too crazed—stripping and washing off with meths will be required.

2. Chemically strip the piece, carefully following the manufacturer's instructions. Safety is paramount when using chemical strippers—wear industrial-strength rubber gloves and safety glasses and work in a well-ventilated area.

3. Neutralise paint stripper by wiping over with methylated spirits soaked in a soft cloth (spirits will also evaporate fast and dry the timber, so you'll be able to work on your piece again straight away).

4. Lightly sand timber surfaces, first with 150-grit sandpaper, then with a finer 240-grit sandpaper to end with a smooth finish. (Always sand with the grain—if you sand against the grain scratches will show through after the finish is applied.)

before

2

3.

4.

5.

6.

8.

7.

9.

5. Fill in any holes with wood stop (in the same colour as the finish). When the filler is dry, lightly sand back with 240-grit sandpaper. Dust off all surfaces.

6. Apply stain evenly to the chair and allow to dry.

7. Apply three coats of shellac by brush, lightly sanding with 400-grit sandpaper between each coat.

8. Prepare for waxing by lightly sanding the topcoat with 400-grit sandpaper and then 00-grade steel wool. This will ensure a smooth, clean surface.

9. Apply wax with 0000-grade steel wool; allow to dry for 15–20 minutes, before burnishing off with a clean, soft cloth.

RE-COVER A DROP SEAT

Drop seats just pop in and out of the chair—and therefore are very easy to re-cover. If the foam and webbing are in good condition, you just need to tear off the old fabric and staple on the new.

However, in this case we needed to replace the foam and webbing as well.

WHAT YOU NEED

Staple gun

Webbing

Foam, cut to size

Glue

Fabric

METHOD

1. Remove old fabric, stuffing and webbing, leaving just the frame intact.

2. Use a staple gun to attach the new webbing. Start by attaching rows running in one direction, and then weave more rows through running in the other direction.

3. Glue the foam onto the frame.

4. Place the frame face-down onto the fabric. Wrap and staple.

2a.

2b.

3.

4.

after

before

Revamping Everyday Pieces

This is where you get to be more daring in your design choices. Transforming a piece from frumpy to fabulous is enormous fun—and it's even more satisfying when it costs next to nothing.

Sanding versus Stripping

Good painting is all in the preparation. Unfortunately, the preparation is tedious, but it must be done, and done well. You can remove old paint by sanding or by chemically stripping. Sanding is generally the easiest option for smaller jobs—however, strippers may be more effective for fiddly areas or when there's a thick build-up of paint.

If you are going to sand a vintage piece of furniture, keep in mind that most paints used until 1970 contained lead, so if you think there's any chance of there being lead paint on the furniture, check before sanding. You can do this by buying a very cheap and simple-to-use lead testing kit at your local paint shop.

I'm cautious of using traditional chemical strippers at home because of their high toxicity; however, there are now some great natural citrus-based strippers on the market, which are much safer to work with. The trick is to neutralise the paint stripper with methylated spirits after you've used it, otherwise the fresh paint won't adhere properly.

VINTAGE KITCHEN CHAIR (HIGH-GLOSS FINISH)

This common vintage kitchen chair was bought at a garage sale for only a few dollars. I know some people would love its 'Shabby Chic' appeal, but it was too rough for me—I love finishes to be smooth and tactile. It was also far too dirty and needed a good clean.

WHAT YOU NEED

Sugar soap and a cloth
Sandpaper
High-gloss water-based enamel

METHOD

1. Clean thoroughly with sugar soap and warm water and allow it to dry.

2. Sand back until smooth and then wipe away any dust.

3. Apply two coats of high-gloss water-based enamel (the higher the gloss, the hardier the paint, which is good for a kitchen chair).

after

before

2a.

2b.

after

Chocolate
mud cup
cakes &
Strawberries
♥!

RAW PINE STOOL (BLACK WOOD WASH)

This little solid pine stool was picked up cheaply from IKEA. The beauty of buying raw pine pieces is that they're so easy to up-cycle. Just ensure that the timber is raw and doesn't have a clear seal on it—and you're good to go.

WHAT YOU NEED

Sandpaper

Black wood wash, paintbrush

Soft cloth

Clear sealer (if a hardier finish is desired)

METHOD

1. Very lightly sand the stool, just enough to allow the wash to stick.

2. Apply the wash with a paintbrush, wiping off any excess with a soft cloth as you go. Repeat this process if a deeper colour is desired.

Tip This will leave a natural matt finish—if you prefer a glossier, hardier surface, seal with an all-purpose clear sealer.

SOFT INDUSTRIAL LOCKER (RUST FINISH)

Vintage industrial furniture adds masculinity and drama to an interior. You can find genuine aged and weather-beaten pieces, but they're generally quite pricey.

A more economical way to achieve this look is to buy a simple locker (ours was purchased from an office supply store) and use specialised paint products to create an authentic rusted iron effect.

The result is utterly divine and the process is simple.

WHAT YOU NEED

Undercoat

A 'rust' base paint

A 'rust' solution/finish

Clear sealer

Brushes and rags

METHOD

1. Roughly sand the locker and apply one coat of undercoat

2. Apply two coats of the rust base paint (we used Porter's Paints Liquid Iron) by brush—allow 12 hours drying time between coats (don't overly worry about how neat your painting is, it won't matter as long as the locker is covered).

3. Apply the rust solution (we used Porter's Instant Rust) when the second coat of base paint is touch dry (you can play around until you reach the level of rust you're happy with—the more instant rust you apply, the more rust you'll get).

4. Allow two days to dry before applying a clear sealer.

1.

2.

3.

after

before

2.

4.

5.

6.

7.

8.

9.

80S-STYLE DESK ('AGED' FINISH)

Anastasia's husband, Jason, restored this old 80s-style desk for her, using two shades of milk paint and beeswax. This technique produces a beautifully 'aged' finish.

The undercoat you get does need to be suitable for milk paint. In this project, Porter's milk paint in Provencale was used as the base colour and Sableux as the second colour.

WHAT YOU NEED

Screwdriver

Sandpaper

Undercoat

Good-quality paintbrushes

2 shades of milk paint, base colour and
    second colour

Beeswax and toothbrush

Spatula and brushes

Fine-grade steel wool

Clear water-based sealer and bamboo
    skewer

Black pigment

METHOD

1. Remove the handles with a screwdriver, sand thoroughly and wipe down.

2. Apply one coat of undercoat with a brush.

3. Apply two coats of your chosen base colour. Sand lightly between coats.

4. Use a toothbrush to apply a small amount of beeswax to the areas you'd like the base colour to show through. It's a good idea to choose areas that will naturally age faster, such as the corners, edges and around the handles.

5. Apply two coats of your second colour of milk paint.

6. Gently scrape waxed areas with a spatula, and then a fine-grade steel wool, to reveal the base colour.

7. To create an aged finish, pour clear sealer into a jar and use a bamboo skewer to add a small amount of black pigment. To mix, shake vigorously with the lid on.

8. Apply two coats of sealer.

9. Screw in new handles.

The best places to source affordable vintage furniture are garage sales, charity shops and by the roadside. Don't look at the tatty old fabric or a bad paint job; look at the shape and structure. You must love the shape from the beginning, as that won't change.

OUTDOOR ROOMS AND KITCHEN GARDENS

Taking it Outside

It's not hard, even in the most humble home, to find a little alfresco nook you can do up gorgeously—all you need is a little time and creative inspiration. And then, to really make the most of your outdoor space, plant a simple kitchen garden and delight in the joy of growing your own food.

Vintage wicker, metal and timber outdoor furniture can all be easily found and revamped with a fresh coat of paint—just remember to use the correct primer on metal furniture. If you need new cushioning, trace the shape you require onto a piece of paper or cardboard and take your template into a foam store to have it cut. It's important to ask for outdoor foam, as regular foam will mould, even if covered in outdoor fabric.

For special occasions, I love to drag indoor furniture out—there's something so decadent about reclining on an upholstered armchair outside. You can also hang beautiful lanterns and chandeliers from a tree, or create fabric tents and scatter floor cushions on the lawn; it's the unexpected that creates an unforgettable luncheon.

Make every meal even more special by adding your own freshly picked herbs and vegies. You don't need a lot of room to start a kitchen garden—a square metre is fine—but you do need a lot of sun. To really flourish, vegetables need around six hours a day.

Sara Breckenridge, a permaculturalist who runs a kitchen garden at my daughter's school, suggests living in a new home for at least a year before planting a permanent kitchen garden—this way you get a chance to track the sun and find the best spot. In the interim, grow a few vegies in pots.

A potted kitchen garden is also a good option if you only have a balcony or small courtyard. Place the pots on castors so you can easily move the plants around to follow the sun.

Opposite: A vivid multi-coloured umbrella entices the viewer outside.

Roses–the Queen of the Flowers

Roses are majestic in the garden, divine as cut flowers, and edible too.

- Ask your local nursery which varieties grow well in your region. Remember to use a good-quality soil, fertilise regularly and prune when dormant.
- Cut roses early in the morning and place immediately into cool water. Use sharp scissors for cutting and cut the stems on a slant. Keep the vase beautifully clean and top up with fresh water daily.
- Organic rose petals can be tossed into salads or sugar-coated for cake decorating.

Make Your Own Compost

Making your own compost is wonderfully beneficial for your garden and for the environment in general.

In an urban environment, the cleanest and most convenient way to compost is to buy a compost bin. Place it nice and close to the kitchen to make it easier to use.

What to compost:

- Fruit and vegetable scraps
- Tea leaves and bags
- Coffee grounds
- Crushed eggshells
- Fresh lawn clippings, twigs and dead leaves
- A little shredded paper (dampen first)

A SIMPLE KITCHEN GARDEN

Once you've picked your spot (north-facing gardens are generally the best), create a raised garden bed to ensure good drainage. You can build a permanent border from sleepers, rocks or other materials; buy a pre-made raised garden bed or create one yourself by up-cycling almost any vintage container.

For example, you could drill holes into the bottom of an antique enamel baby's bath or take the bottom off a French champagne crate and place it straight on the ground. It doesn't really matter what you use as a container or border, as long as it allows plenty of drainage.

WHAT YOU NEED

Garden soil

Compost

Organic mulch (lucerne is good)

Seedlings

Trowel, fork, gloves and watering can

(all of the above supplies should be readily available from your local nursery)

Fertiliser (fish emulsion is good)

METHOD

1. Add soil to the garden bed. Healthy soil means healthy plants; so buy the best you can afford.

2. Mix some good-quality compost through the soil (you need about one-third compost to two-thirds soil).

3. Spread with a thin layer of organic mulch (to help keep the soil moist).

4. Plant your seedlings.

5. Water well. Feed regularly with fertiliser.

Garden Tips

- If you're placing your kitchen garden border directly onto lawn, put down a layer of damp newspaper first to suppress weed growth.

- It's important to water your garden regularly, but be careful not to over-water it. You can test whether your garden needs watering or not by poking your finger into the soil. Ideally the soil needs to be damp, not wet and not dry. It's always best to water your plants early in the morning.

- Regularly feed your plants with a little fish emulsion or other quality fertiliser.

- Just a few vegies, a few herbs and a lemon tree are enough to make a substantial difference to the way you eat. If your garden isn't big enough for a lemon tree, try planting one of the dwarf varieties in a pot.

- Scatter some lavender and marigolds through your garden, they'll help repel pests and look pretty.

Five Easy-To-Grow Vegetables

Beans

Beetroot

Capsicum

Lettuce

Tomatoes

Five Easy-To-Grow Herbs

Basil

Mint

Parsley

Rosemary

Thyme

2a.

2b.

4.

after

MILKY TERRACOTTA POTS

A lived-in garden is infinitely more appealing, and one way to create the impression a garden has been around for some time is to 'age' the pots.

Terracotta pots naturally whiten with age and become beautifully covered in moss. There are ways to hasten this process with yoghurt or buttermilk, but it's a little messy and smelly, so I prefer to tone down the bright orange of new terracotta pots with milk paint instead.

WHAT YOU NEED

Terracotta pot (ensure it has drainage
    holes in the bottom)
White milk paint
Paint brush and sandpaper
Potting mix
Seedlings

METHOD

1. Paint the outside of the pot with white milk paint.

2. Lightly sand back until you get the desired effect.

3. Fill the pot three-quarters full with a good-quality potting mix.

4. Plant your seedlings.

Terracotta Tip

Terracotta is very porous, which means the pots dry out quickly and plants need to be watered much more frequently. To help retain the water, cut up an old plastic bag and line the inside sides of the pot before filling with soil. Leave the bottom unlined for drainage.

Recipes

Herb Butter

INGREDIENTS

Parsley, oregano and any other herbs of
 your choice
Organic full-cream butter, softened

METHOD

1. Finely chop the herbs and mix them through the butter.

2. Generously spread herb butter on fresh, crusty rolls. Eat as is, or wrap the rolls in aluminium foil and bake in a moderate oven for 10–15 minutes.

TIP You might also like to try herb butter with hot corn-on-the-cob.

Pesto

INGREDIENTS

A bunch of basil or rocket (about two cups)

$^1/_3$ of a cup of macadamia nuts

$^1/_3$ of a cup of grated parmesan

3 cloves of garlic, roughly chopped

1 cup of extra virgin olive oil

METHOD

1. If you have a food processor, simply add all the ingredients except for the olive oil, which you drizzle in slowly with the motor running. However, if you want to make pesto with a blender, I find you need to use more olive oil. Pour three quarters of the cup of oil in before you turn on the blender (otherwise it won't want to go at all)—then drizzle in the final quarter of the cup once the motor is running.

2. Pesto is, of course, fabulous with pasta, but it's also good on bread or as a dip. Store any leftover pesto in a jar in the fridge, and add a layer of olive oil to the top of the pesto to help preserve it.

TIP: It's more traditional to add pine nuts to pesto, but I love to use Australian macadamia nuts instead. Locally sourced nuts will also be fresher, which is quite important, as nuts tend to go rancid fairly quickly. As does olive oil, so again, choose local over imported.

Baked Baby Tomatoes

INGREDIENTS

Baby tomatoes

A few sprigs of thyme

Salt and pepper

Extra virgin olive oil

METHOD

1. Place tomatoes in a baking tray and add thyme, salt and pepper. Generously drizzle with olive oil and gently toss.

2. Bake in a moderate 350°F (180°C) oven for 10–15 minutes, or until softened.

Pear, Walnut and Feta Salad

INGREDIENTS

A bunch of rocket

One pear, thinly sliced

A few slices of Spanish onion

A handful of walnuts

A handful of feta, cubed

A little olive oil

Juice of ½ a lemon

Salt and pepper, to taste

METHOD

1. Toss all ingredients together and drizzle with olive oil. Season with lemon and salt and pepper as desired.

Mint Tea

INGREDIENTS

One teaspoon of mint leaves
A pot of boiling water

METHOD

1. Pick mint leaves straight from your garden and let them steep for 10 minutes in a pot of boiling water. Use a strainer to pour into a teacup.

TIP: You can also try chamomile, lemongrass or ginger root. Add lemon and/or honey as desired.

Glossary

ARCHITRAVES: decorative timber mouldings around doors and window frames

BRADAWL: a small, sharp tool used to mark or make a pilot hole

COMPOST: a rich mixture of decaying organic matter used to improve soil quality

CORNICE: a protruding decorative feature joining the top of the wall to the ceiling

'CUTTING IN': a brush technique used to paint into the corners and edges of walls.

EO PARTICLEBOARD (ULTRA LOW-EMISSION PARTICLEBOARD): a more eco-friendly alternative to MDF and other particleboards. EO particleboards only contain a small amount of formaldehyde

GARDEN CLOCHE: a covered frame used to protect delicate plants and seedlings from wildlife and weather

LOW-E GLASS (LOW-EMISSIVITY GLASS): regular glass with a metal oxide coating applied, which helps to reduce heat passing through the window

MDF (MEDIUM-DENSITY FIBREBOARD): a board made primarily from wood fibres, which have been glued together under pressure and heat. MDF contains formaldehydes, so safety gear should be worn when cutting into it

MULCH: a layer of grass clippings, dried leaves or shredded prunings used to suppress weed growth and help the soil retain moisture

PELMETS: a decorative top, which hides the top of the curtain. Pelmets are usually made from timber covered in fabric

PENDANTS: any hanging light fitting

PRIMER: the first coat of paint, which is used to seal and protect the substrate

SISAL RUGS: made from the fibres extracted from the Agave plant, sisal rugs are eco-friendly and naturally dust-mite resistant

STEEL WOOL (GRADES): steel wool is graded from 0000 to 4—with 0000 being the finest and used for the likes of wax polishing and 4 being the coarsest and used for heavy duty stripping

SUBSTRATE: the surface below the finish surface, which provides support for the finish surface

TRAVERTINE: popular in Italian architecture, travertine is a form of limestone deposited by springs

UNDERCOAT: the second coat of paint. Its purpose is to stick to the primer (or existing wall paint when no primer is required) and fill any minor defects, leaving a smooth, non-porous surface for the topcoat

WOODSTOP: a water-based filler for wood, comes in a variety of colours.

Acknowledgements

Firstly I'd like to thank my friend Anastasia for her stunningly beautiful photographs—and for being a joy to work with.

We'd both like to thank all the wonderful homeowners (and their families) who graciously allowed us to shoot their homes; Tess Wells, Stephen Pellegrino, Elizabeth Sachs, Kelli Zakharoff, Fleur Madden (and decorator, Tracy Madden), Janine Tucker, Amber Hawkins, Vanessa Scoon and Kellie Armstrong—and some of my lovely clients who did the same; Sonia Wakefield, Erica Davis and Susan Corley—and we'd also love to thank Marietjie Brown for inviting us into her beautiful garden.

We're so grateful to all the tradespeople and artisans who generously shared their time and knowledge with us; Andrew Baxter from Baxter's Antique Restorations, who is a master craftsman and taught us so much; Jane Wilson for her friendship and sewing; Denise Kennedy from Curtain Elegance who selflessly shared her trade secrets with us; Deborah Johnston-Booker from Johnston-Booker Faux-Finish for her painting advice; Graham Daniels from G. S. Daniels and Co. for his wallpapering advise; Tristan Mathieson from Austimber Floor Sanding for his flooring advice and Sara Breckenridge for her wonderful gardening advice.

It would have been hard to complete all our projects without the product support from the following companies; Porter's Paints; Mokum; Warwick Fabrics; Westbury Textiles; Clark Rubber, Lincraft and Livos Australia. Thank you so much.

We'd also like to thank designer KT Doyle and Moore & Moore Wallpapers, Parry and Williams, Side Street Vintage and wood turner Lee Wilson—and all the stores/businesses who let me raid them for props; Blake & Taylor, Basil Bangs, Twig and Grace, Moose & Bird, House and Doll, Industrial Revolution at The Woollangabba Antique Centre, Sachs and Cornish at the Paddington Antique Centre and especially Anka at Les Salles.

A huge thank you to the team at New Holland, in particular our publisher Lliane Clarke who has been so enthusiastic and supportive and our project editor Jodi De Vantier who is just so lovely to work with.

Also, a special thanks to my beloved father who taught me to appreciate good workmanship and the concept of quality—and to Anastasia's husband Jason who generously helped us with some of our projects—and to our little models; Emily, Scarlett and Saska.

This edition published in 2013 by
New Holland Publishers Pty Ltd
London • Sydney • Cape Town • Auckland

www.newhollandpublishers.com

Garfield House 86–88 Edgware Road London W2 2EA United Kingdom
1/66 Gibbes Street Chatswood NSW 2067 Australia
Wembley Square First Floor Solan Road Gardens Cape Town 8001 South Africa
218 Lake Road Northcote Auckland New Zealand

First published in 2011.
Copyright © 2011, 2013 in text: Tahn Scoon
Copyright © 2011, 2013 in photos: Anastasia Kariofyllidis
Copyright © 2011, 2013 New Holland Publishers (Australia) Pty Ltd

A catalogue record of this book is available at the British Library and the National Library of Australia.

ISBN: 9781742574264

Managing Director: Fiona Schultz
Project Editor: Jodi De Vantier
Designer: Celeste Vlok
Cover design: Tracy Loughlin
Photography: Anastasia Kariofyllidis
Production Manager: Olga Dementiev
Printer: Toppan Leefung Printing Ltd (China)

10 9 8 7 6 5 4 3 2 1
Follow New Holland Publishers on
Facebook: www.facebook.com/NewHollandPublishers

WALLPAPER AND FABRIC CREDITS

Wallpaper
P46 – 'Perroquet' by Nina Campbell
P58 – 'Manaus' by Nina Campbell
P68 – 'Ticking Stripe' by Moore & Moore
P77, 132 – 'Marrakesh' by Arte
P137 – 'Curator' by Andrew Martin
P138 – 'Circus' by Catherine Martin

Fabric
P98, 99, 102 – Selection of Mokum fabrics
P101 – 'Alhambra' in Onyx by Warwick
P113 – 'Petite Trianon' in Red Coral by Mokum
P116- 'Dauphine' in Dusk by Mokum
P119 – 'Icarus' in Charcoal by Warwick
P120 – 'Agra' in Riviera by Warwick
P129 – 'Edo Linen' in Truffle by Mokum
P144, 145 – 'Mica' in Cigar by Mokum
P171 – 'Ironwork' in Ebony and Ivory by Westbury